CAMBRIDGE LIBRARY COLLECTION

Books of enduring scholarly value

British and Irish History, Nineteenth Century

This series comprises contemporary or near-contemporary accounts of the political, economic and social history of the British Isles during the nineteenth century. It includes material on international diplomacy and trade, labour relations and the women's movement, developments in education and social welfare, religious emancipation, the justice system, and special events including the Great Exhibition of 1851.

Appearances

This interesting piece of social history, published in 1899, appears to have been the first non-fiction work by Teresa Praga (d.1920), the wife of a portrait painter and miniaturist, who also published novels. Her later output included books on cookery, housekeeping and dress, many with the emphasis on 'easy' (*Easy French Sweets for English Cooks*, for example). Like Jane Panton (several of whose books on lifestyle are also reissued in this series), Praga is writing for middle-class wives with not much money, and aspirations to gracious living. *Appearances* (subtitled *How to Keep Them Up on a Limited Income*) is presented as autobiography: how a newly married woman, on a very restricted income but used to – and liking – being 'waited on', manages a house. With detailed descriptions of finances, menus, the duties of servants, and other minutiae, this is a light-hearted account of late Victorian housekeeping.

T0382370

Cambridge University Press has long been a pioneer in the reissuing of out-of-print titles from its own backlist, producing digital reprints of books that are still sought after by scholars and students but could not be reprinted economically using traditional technology. The Cambridge Library Collection extends this activity to a wider range of books which are still of importance to researchers and professionals, either for the source material they contain, or as landmarks in the history of their academic discipline.

Drawing from the world-renowned collections in the Cambridge University Library and other partner libraries, and guided by the advice of experts in each subject area, Cambridge University Press is using state-of-the-art scanning machines in its own Printing House to capture the content of each book selected for inclusion. The files are processed to give a consistently clear, crisp image, and the books finished to the high quality standard for which the Press is recognised around the world. The latest print-on-demand technology ensures that the books will remain available indefinitely, and that orders for single or multiple copies can quickly be supplied.

The Cambridge Library Collection brings back to life books of enduring scholarly value (including out-of-copyright works originally issued by other publishers) across a wide range of disciplines in the humanities and social sciences and in science and technology.

Appearances

How to Keep Them Up on a Limited Income

Teresa Praga

CAMBRIDGE
UNIVERSITY PRESS

CAMBRIDGE
UNIVERSITY PRESS

University Printing House, Cambridge, CB2 8BS, United Kingdom

Cambridge University Press is part of the University of Cambridge.

It furthers the University's mission by disseminating knowledge in the pursuit of
education, learning and research at the highest international levels of excellence.

www.cambridge.org
Information on this title: www.cambridge.org/9781108071925

© in this compilation Cambridge University Press 2014

This edition first published 1899
This digitally printed version 2014

ISBN 978-1-108-07192-5 Paperback

This book reproduces the text of the original edition. The content and language reflect
the beliefs, practices and terminology of their time, and have not been updated.

Cambridge University Press wishes to make clear that the book, unless originally published
by Cambridge, is not being republished by, in association or collaboration with,
or with the endorsement or approval of, the original publisher or its successors in title.

Appearances

APPEARANCES

How to Keep them up on a
Limited Income

BY

Mrs. Alfred Praga

Author of
" Dinners of the Day," " Starting 'House-Keeping," etc.

London

John Long

6 Chandos Street, Strand
1899

CONTENTS

Contents

INTRODUCTION

WE loved each other dearly, but—there is always a but, and in our case it was a very big one. Our worldly wealth stood exactly as follows :—

Item, £150 in the bank.

Item, an income, which, allowing for fluctuations totalled out at but £300 a year.

These were our advantages. The disadvantages were that we were both gentle folk, that we liked things—by which, I mean our surroundings—fresh, decent, and in order. That we preferred meals daintily cooked, and well served ; and, that biggest obstacle of all, we both liked, nay had been accustomed to, being "waited on."

Also, the fact is an unromantic one, nevertheless as truth must prevail let me duly set it forth, we had both of us the most prosaic appetites imaginable ; healthy, hearty appetites, which, fond as we were, and are, of each other, resolutely refused to be put off with a diet of bread and cheese, indeed revolted at the bare idea, promise to flavour it, as we might, with kisses. In addition to all this, "appearances" would have to be "kept up."

"You must wait," said Wisdom in the guise of our respective fathers and mothers.

But when did two young and loving hearts ever want to wait yet ? and we were no exception to the

I

rule. In effect we said so, and were met with the retort from my mother that nowadays it was impossible to get a decent house-parlourmaid under £18 a year, and, from *his* father, that untold numbers of young professional men had ruined their careers and ended in the gutter by injudicious early marriages.

For a minute—perhaps a minute and a half—we were daunted.

Then we faced the situation boldly, and finding that we met with but scant sympathy and positively *no* encouragement from our elders, we resolved to face it together.

"£300 a year," said he pensively, nibbling the end of a pen.

"£300 a year," echoed I, gazing dolefully at the sheet of unsullied paper lying before us.

Then a bright idea struck me. "Let us map it out," I suggested.

"The first thing to be thought about is the house." This was, so to speak simultaneous.

"I should be sorry to see *my* child living in a—a *low* neighbourhood," observed mother, on the brink of tears.

"The only place I know of where you'd be at all likely to get a decent house at a moderate rental is Bedford Park," interjected his father, "and I've heard that the drainage there is far from perfect," he added gloomily.

"Bedford Park is too far off," asserted we, together.

"And too dull," I added, "nobody would ever come to see us."

"Of course if you mean to give dinner parties," said my mother.

"On three hundred a year!" added his father sarcastically.

Here I lost my temper. I am always the first to lose my temper. I may as well tell the reader that at once, and get the confession over.

Well, the upshot of it all was that we mapped things out, and the result of that mapping, and how it worked, is here within this little volume, to be of service, I hope, to those similarly placed.

CHAPTER I

WAYS AND MEANS ON £300 A YEAR

£300 a year isn't, I admit, a very large sum, especially when it has to provide not only house, food, firing and lights, but clothing, amusements, pocket money, and all the hundred and one incidental expenses of daily life besides.

The first thing to be thought of, we agreed, as we had previously done, was to find a house.

Kensington was too dear; Fulham too fifth-rate; Hammersmith too noisy; Ravenscourt Park too far off. Bedford Park also came under the latter category. Finally we decided upon West Kensington, and after much searching we were fortunate enough to discover "just what we wanted," in a road which almost faced the station, and past whose corner went 'busses to every imaginable part of London.

This house was one of a row all like itself. It had what is euphemistically known as "a good entrance," being flanked on either side with solid looking pillars, and boasting a portico (a priceless blessing in some people's eyes, I believe). To describe it properly, I will begin with the basement. Here there was the usual area, with coal cellars, dustbin, etc.; a kitchen of very fair size, a breakfast room ditto, and a scullery with a copper. When I saw that copper I hesitated no longer.

4

It turned the balance, because I knew that by its aid the one item I dreaded could be kept at bay. I refer to the washing bill.

In addition to the scullery was a yard, dreary enough perhaps, and of the usual London pattern, " Quite good enough though to dry clothes in," I mentally decided.

But to go on. On the ground floor was a good sized dining-room, and at the back another room, which would form an admirable study or smoking den. Upstairs was the drawing-room, not by any manner of means a pokey apartment, capable indeed of accommodating forty or fifty people at an evening party quite comfortably. It was splendidly lighted, too, having in addition to the bay, another French window, which opened on to a balcony.

Upstairs again there were four good bedrooms, a dressing-room, with marble lavatory fitment, a bath-room, with hot and cold water, and the usual offices. And for all this they were asking but a modest £50 yearly. " On three years' agreement," added the obliging young man who was showing us over.

" It's a big slice out of "—said " he " dubiously. The sentence remained unfinished, but I knew what was meant.

" You see, little woman, there's the taxes to go on to that." The " young man " caught the word " Taxes," and thinking doubtless we were but ignorant young things, interjected complacently, " One-third of the rent, I think you'll find, sir."

But I didn't mean to give up the chance of owning that copper without a struggle. " We'll

5

make an offer," I whispered determinedly. " If we take it for twenty-one years, I bet they'll let us have it for £40 a year," and as a matter of fact they did. Further, we got a clause put into the lease by which we could " determine it " at seven or fourteen years.

Before we finally decided to take the house we called into requisition an expert opinion as to the drains, etc., and had them thoroughly tested. The sanitary engineer's fee for doing this was a guinea, but money spent in such a cause should never be begrudged, as it is the one and only means of avoiding perhaps very serious illness.

We were also careful to see that a clause was inserted in our lease whereby the landlord and not ourselves was liable for the repairs. A repairing lease is a terrible clog round the neck when means are in any way limited, and I would advise the reader never to burden his or herself with one, or they will be bound to regret it sooner or later.

The taxes, as they originally stood, came to some £18 per year, but guided by my husband's legal knowledge we appealed against this at the quin-quennial assessment*, fortunately just then coming on, on the ground that the house was overrated in proportion to the rent paid for it, and we were thus fortunate enough to get them reduced, so that with water, rates, etc., all told, our taxes only came to just £15. This left us in hand with precisely £245.

* This assessment is only held once in every five years, but it is possible to appeal to the Committee of Assessment at any time on the ground that a house is overrated.

The next serious item to claim our attention was the question of the coal bill.

Now we love big fires, both of us, and moreover, in winter, are partial to one in our bedroom. "It is cheaper and better in the long run," said I firmly, "to pay the coal merchant than the doctor. With those big grates and big rooms we sha'n't be able to do with much less than a ton a month, taking the summer and winter together, and over-cheap coals are the dearest in the end; no, I really don't think we can say less than £12 for coals."

"And for gas?" queried he.

"Well, we both *love* sitting up late, don't we?" My lord and master assented. "Then I think we must allow eight pounds for the gas bill, and if we can get it under that, well, so much the better, and it will be so much money saved, won't it?"

This was incontrovertible, so we put down on our "table of expenses," coals £12, gas £8.

"It only leaves £225," said he ruefully.

"A perfect fortune," I answered gaily.

"But the servants' wages," he asked doubtfully.

"£10 a year for the cook, £5 for the housemaid," I made reply.

"And that will leave you with just £210 in hand," he cried somewhat aghast.

"Very well," said I promptly. "Then you must give me a hundred and four pounds a year for the household expenses; that works out at just £2 a week, and leaves you with a hundred and six pounds a year. The six pounds you must bank, we'll save that."

"And the £100."

7

"The hundred is to provide our clothes, travelling expenses, pocket money, and annual holidays. You must give me an allowance," I added. "I think £25 a year will be about fair, and then I shall always have money in my pocket, and sha'n't have to go worrying to you for every little thing I want, from a 'bus fare to a pair of stockings."

"It won't be enough," he urged.

"It will have to be," said I firmly. "You forget that men's clothes cost more than women's, and then you *must* always have money in your pocket ; and you forget, too, that you've always got to pay for me wherever we go." Finally we settled it on this basis. And now I'm going to tell you how it all worked out. How we furnished doesn't matter ; suffice it to say that it cost us just a hundred guineas all told, and I may add, without vanity, that ours is one of the prettiest houses I've ever seen. You see, we didn't make the fatal mistake of overcrowding the rooms with furniture, and we didn't go in for hangings of any sort, except the harmless necessary short and long curtains.

First and foremost, because I believe hangings of all sorts are more or less unhealthy ; and, secondly, because, unless one wishes one's house to have a tawdry, ill-kempt, *and* ill-kept appearance, these things add to that bugbear—the washing bill—to no inconsiderable extent. As a matter of fact, I've no long washing curtains at all, except in the bedrooms, and those are of "art linen," *bien entendu.*

8

CHAPTER II

As soon as we were married, and had got our house in decent order, I set about finding the servants wherewith to " run it."

Most of our relatives by the way were, or professed themselves to be, perfectly aghast at my decision to keep two. It was " absurd," " extravagant," " unnecessary," " ostentation," and a host of other things it will serve no purpose to chronicle here.

For myself I went the even tenor of my way quite undisturbed by these criticisms. I knew well enough that in a house (I say nothing of flats), such as I wished ours to be, there could be no real comfort, no good cooking, unless I was prepared to degenerate into a household drudge and do it all myself—in one comprehensive word, no daintiness, unless we could keep two domestics, and therefore I determined that by hook or by crook two I would have.

"It isn't the wages, it's the food," said my mother in a portentous voice, but I was deaf even to maternal counsel. So one bright morning, donning my prettiest hat, I set forth in search of what all my women friends assured me was the unattainable.

I knew that the dear Sisters at Nazareth House, Hammersmith, had several hundred children under

9

their care, and I hoped to find among these one of a suitable age to take a first situation.

Fortune favoured me, for the Reverend Mother, after I had explained that I wished to take a young girl to train as house-parlourmaid, but could not pay more than two shillings per week, sent in for my inspection a tall, slim strip of a girl who though but just past her fourteenth birthday looked a good three or four years older, and, after promising to look well after her, to see that she attended to her religious duties with unfailing regularity, and not to allow her out late at night, I was allowed to engage her. Thus my initial difficulty was over. I promised to provide her with caps and smart aprons, these latter to remain my property in the event of her leaving, and then, after settling what day she should enter, I took my departure, highly pleased with myself.

The next thing to be done was to find a cook. "A cook for ten pounds a year," said my mother-in-law pityingly; "well, I don't want to dishearten you, dear, but I don't think you'll get her."

However, nothing daunted, I advertised in a country paper as follows: "Wanted, a strong girl, aged eighteen to twenty; must be able to do plain cooking, light place, two in family, house-parlour-maid kept. Wages, £10 per annum." I had three replies. Two from girls who had never been out before, one from a girl who had been a sort of general servant to a family living in Oxford, but who was anxious to obtain a London place. Fortunately for me she was coming on a visit to some friends in town, so that an interview was easily arranged. When she made her appearance, I first questioned her closely as to whether she liked, *really* liked, cooking, "because if you do," said I, "I can soon train you to be a very good cook, otherwise it's no use my engaging you."

However, fortunately she did like cooking, and she did not object to washing; so after explaining with the utmost explicity and thoroughness exactly what her duties would be, I engaged her, and so delighted was I with my efforts that I took the earliest possible opportunity of informing our respective families of the success which had attended my servant hunting.

I regret to say that my announcement was, to say the least of it, sceptically received.

"You'll never make anything of them," said my mother.

"I should look after the glass and china myself if I were you," said *his* mother. "I know those young girls. They're dreadful 'breakers,' all of them."

Well, it may have been due to the perversity of human nature, but then and there I vowed to myself that I would turn my "raw material" into two first-class servants; and I did.

For the benefit of those similarly placed I will explain my methods.

CHAPTER III

FIRST and foremost then I must tell you that up to now we had been dependent upon the services of a charwoman, who, for a consideration, had consented to come in and " do " for us pending the arrival of our domestics. She used to prepare breakfast and lunch, and after washing up the luncheon things, left us for the rest of the day while she went to make some other family " comfortable."

Our dinner we took at restaurants, a different one every night, but we were rapidly growing tired of this, because expensive restaurants were of course beyond our means, and even the cheaper ones made the money fly a good deal faster than we either of us liked. I had arranged that our new servants should enter on the Monday evening, and during the whole of the day I was busy, aided by Mrs. Charwoman, who restored everything to a state of exquisite cleanliness and order, my own part of the work being as follows :—

First I made a list of the entire contents of the linen press, then of the glass and china cupboards, and finally of the silver—most of it was electro by the way—but that to me mattered nothing. This done, I made a duplicate copy of each list in a little penny book, to be handed to my new maid when she should arrive. I had previously purchased two large sheets of white cardboard and upon these I drew up a list of the duties I expected each maid to perform, dividing them into " Every-day Duties " and " Special Duties." This is how I apportioned out the work of our modest establishment :—

COOK'S DUTIES.

MORNINGS.

Light kitchen fire.

Sweep hall, dining-room, study, and lavatory. If needful clean grates and light fires.

While dust settles, clean door-steps and brasses.

Dust hall, dining-room, study, and lavatory.

Prepare and have own breakfast.

Prepare dining-room breakfast.

Tidy kitchen.

Take orders for day.

Attend to special duties for day.

Prepare lunch for kitchen and dining-room.

After lunch : Wash up.

Clean kitchen.

Tidy scullery.

Attend to special duties if any.

Have own tea.

After tea : Prepare dining-room dinner. Afterwards have own dinner. Wash up. Tidy kitchen and scullery for night.

SPECIAL DUTIES.

Mondays.—Do washing. Clothes to be put to soak on Sunday night.

Tuesdays.—Clean all brasses and kitchen brights. Turn out store cupboards and pantries.

Wednesdays.—Do ironing and own mending.

Thursdays.—Turn out dining-room. Housemaid helps.

Fridays.—Turn out study, hall, lavatory, and servants' bedroom.

13

Saturdays.—Turn out and clean thoroughly kitchen, scullery, area passages and steps, and sweep yard.

Be dressed by four o'clock.

Nights out, every other Sunday. One evening per week.

The house-parlourmaid's duties I arranged as follows :—

HOUSE PARLOURMAID'S DUTIES.

MORNINGS.

Sweep and dust stairs. Take hot water, tea and letters to mistress's bed-room.

Take hot water to master's dressing-room.

Sweep and dust drawing-room.

Clean boots and knives.

Lay dining-room breakfast, and kitchen ditto.

Have own breakfast.

Serve dining-room breakfast.

Strip beds. Empty slops. Make beds. Sweep and dust bed-rooms and bath-room.

Wash up breakfast things. Clean knives.

Attend to special duties for the day. Lay kitchen and dining-room lunch. Dress. Wait at dining-room lunch.

Have own lunch.

After lunch : Clear away dining-room and kitchen luncheon things, and wash up all silver, glass, and china.

Clean knives. Attend to special duties for the day.

Make and serve afternoon tea. Lay kitchen tea. Have own tea.

After tea : Wash up all tea things, silver, etc.

Lay dining-room and kitchen dinner. Take hot water to bed and dressing-rooms.

Serve dining-room dinner and wait at table.

After dining-room dinner : Have own dinner.

Clear away dining-room dinner things, and wash up all glass, silver, and china.

Tidy bedrooms for night. Turn down beds. Take hot water to bedrooms.

SPECIAL DUTIES.

Mondays.—Do all house mending.

Tuesdays.—Turn out drawing-room.

Wednesdays.—Clean glass cupboard and all the silver.

Thursdays.—Turn out spare bedrooms.

Fridays.—Turn out mistress's bed-room and dressing-room.

Saturdays.—Do mistress's mending.

Be dressed by One o'clock.

Nights out.—

By adopting this plan I did away at once with any chance of disputes between my two hench-women. You see they *cannot* very well quarrel as to " my work " or " your work," when their mistress's commands in black and white are staring them out of countenance.

One of these cards then—the cook's—I nailed up behind the kitchen door. The other I secured to the door of the glass cupboard.

By this time the maids had arrived, and after showing them their bed-room, I gave them just time to take off their things, and then took them a tour of the house; finally, after giving cook her orders for the next day's breakfast, I told them that as they would find all their work clearly written out, there was no need to detain them any longer, so they went, and I sat down, tired out, but triumphant.

15

CHAPTER IV

DOMESTIC DETAILS—HOW IT WORKED

THE next morning before I gave my orders, I explained to cook that I intended to send in, every Saturday, sufficient stores to last the week out. "I always allowance my servants," said I, pleasantly—I omitted to add that they two were the first servants of my "very own" I had ever had—"because I find it works so much better, and then I always know exactly how much is required. I shall allow you quarter of a pound of tea, a pound of sugar, and half a pound of butter each. I only allow the same quantity for your master and myself, so you see you are being treated with absolute fairness. I expect all these, and whatever other stores I send in, to last the whole week," I went on, "and if there is any deficiency I shall expect you to make it good. Of course I always make an extra allowance when we have a luncheon or dinner party," I concluded, feeling horribly mean, and quite expecting my newly-acquired domestic treasure to give notice on the spot, and yet, after mature deliberation, this was the only plan I could think of to make her sufficiently careful. However, she only smiled, and said pleasantly—

"Oh! I'll make them last all right, ma'am." So taking heart of grace I followed up my advantage. "You must save all the fat from the top of the soup and the joints," I went on, " and once a week we will clarify it, and then it will be fit for use as a frying medium. Do you know how to clarify fat?" She didn't. I made a mental note: Teach her to clarify fat and make stock, as a starting-point."

"Never mind," said I aloud, "I'll show you. It's very simple, and quite easily done."

"Thank you, ma'am," said my Abigail, whom by this time I was quite beginning to like.

"Just one thing more," said I.

"Never throw away anything, no matter if it's only a bit of cold cabbage or potato, or a scrap of bacon rind, until you've shown it to me. When I've trained you, and turned you into a good cook, as I hope to do, why of course it will be quite different. You can use your own discretion then, but in these, your learning days, you must come to me with everything." After this I left her to cook her first lunch for us in undisturbed peace.

Perhaps the reader may wonder why, so let me explain.

To begin with I wanted to find out exactly how much Penelope—her name was Penelope—actually did, or didn't know, and as I could only do this by leaving her for the nonce to herself, I adopted that plan and indulged for once in the extravagance of a hot luncheon; I was far too fond of my husband to wish to experiment on *him*.

I next proceeded to interview my budding house-parlourmaid. I think I have said before that she was a girl of good appearance, and she certainly had pretty manners, as indeed have most of the convent bred children I have ever met.

But I could see at a glance that her ideas of waiting at table and of a parlourmaid's work in general were practically nil. Nothing daunted, though, I set to my task.

"Now, Mary," said I brightly, "I've written all your work out for you, as you see, so that you know *what* you have to do, and now I'm going to tell you just how to do it. I want you to pay great attention to me, and try and remember all I tell you."

"Yes, m'm," she answered in a timid whisper.

"Oh, that won't do," said I cheerily. "You can speak louder than that I know. Say, 'Yes, Madam,' so that I can hear you."

"Yes, Madam," said she, speaking up bravely.

"That's better," I observed in my kindest manner.

"Now I'm going to sit at this table"—we were in the dining-room—"and I want you to imagine that I'm having my dinner, and that you're bringing me the vegetables. Now upon which side would you hand them?" She didn't know, so I told her "the left, always the left." Next between us we laid the cloth, and I explained just where everything had to be put, and showed her the existing difference between fish knives and fruit knives, and exactly how much water must be allowed to each finger bowl. As soon as the table had been laid to my satisfaction, I made her strip it all off again, fold away the table cloth and the serviettes in their native creases, and then all over again *da capo*.

She did this four or five times. The first two or three times she made mistakes, but the fourth and fifth were quite faultless, greatly to her delight and mine!

(The flowers of course I arranged myself, though in time she learnt to do that also.) Before dismissing her, I showed her how to lay the side table, for I had no intention of having my pretty table centres and cloth spoilt by having the dishes, etc., placed on the dinner table itself, and as I knew a joint with us would be a rare occurrence, carving was not a *sine quâ non* in my parlourmaid's education.

"You will have to serve the soup," I warned her, "so you must be careful not to fill the plates too full."

Then I let her go, and I am bound to say our first dinner passed off without a *contretemps* of any kind. True, she made one or two little mistakes, as was perhaps but natural, but nothing serious or glaring marred the harmony of our meal, and my husband was both surprised and delighted.

The reader may perhaps wonder at my adopting the above fashion with an absolutely ignorant, untrained servant; but I had argued the whole matter out with myself thoroughly, and had come to the conclusion that if ever we wanted to indulge in such a luxury as a small dinner party and desired it to go off with due *éclat*, my one and only course was to begin as I meant to go on, and set about turning my little convent girl into a good waitress as speedily as possible. To this end I had her in

APPEARANCES

to wait *en grand tenue* at every meal, with the sole
exception of breakfast, when her duties as housemaid occupied her.

At first my husband, man-like, was inclined to
object to this.

"Surely," he expostulated, "we can have the
things on the table, and wait on ourselves when
we're alone." But I soon convinced him to the
contrary.

"Certainly," said I, "if when you wish to bring
a man home to dinner, you will promise me not to
feel mortified at Mary's clumsiness, for clumsy she
certainly *will* be, unless I accustom her to wait
every evening when we're alone; and above all,"
I went on, "you must promise not to grumble
afterwards."

He was silent, so I continued.

"You see, dear," said I gently, "it would be
quite different if we could afford a thoroughly
trained parlourmaid. It would not matter then
whether we were waited upon or not, because as
she would be *au fait* with all her duties, we could
rely upon her when we wish to entertain. As it is,"
I paused expressively, then went on again, "you
know, I want you to feel that you can bring a
friend, or even a couple of friends, home to dinner
at any time without consulting me beforehand.
I'm not going to pay you such a bad compliment as
to make a better dinner or a prettier table for
strangers than I do for you." That last argument
was convincing, and I heard no more objections
to Mary's presence.

For the benefit of those readers who like

appearances and are wishful of keeping them up, I will explain exactly how I managed matters.

We will take the following as a specimen *menu** :—

Bouillon á l'oignon.

Fried fresh herrings.   Mustard sauce.

Mutton cutlets à la firval.   Butter beans à la française.

Vienna pudding.

The side table was laid as usual—we always used the half-soiled dinner cloths folded in three for this purpose, as it helped to keep down the washing bill, and the side table being out of the glare of the light, the cloth did not show so much—with a plentitude of clean forks, spoons, etc., and the bread platter and loaf in case we should need more bread.   I had this cut in the room to save waste.

Cook having brought the soup and soup plates to the dining-room door, where Mary took them from her, they were placed on the side table ; she then served the soup.

When we were alone I instructed her to fill the plates, as there is nothing to equal a plateful of good soup for taking the edge off even the keenest appetite, but when we were entertaining guests of course the plates were only filled in the usual manner, *i.e.* three parts full.   The soup disposed of, she rang the bell to let cook know we were ready for the next course, then cleared away the plates and took in the fish, which by this time had arrived at the dining-room door, placed the dish containing it on a tiny waiter which we kept for the purpose,

* Recipes appended later.

and which was just large enough to accommodate it, together with the sauce boat containing the sauce, and then handed it in the approved fashion, afterwards seeing to the wine, bread, etc. We made it a rule always to have claret, even though we took but a solitary glass apiece, because I wanted my little maid to get into the way of drawing corks, and serving wine, etc., properly.

The fish finished she rang the bell again, and when the *entrée* arrived—in this instance it was garnished with vegetables, so that only one dish was needed—handed that, and again saw to the bread, etc., and when the vegetable *entrée* and pudding made their appearance respectively, the process I have indicated above was repeated.

The pudding disposed of, she took a small waiter and removed the salts, pepperettes, etc., then with the crumb scoop and tray removed the crumbs, set a fruit plate garnished with a d'oyley, finger bowl and fruit knife and fork in front of each of us, handed the fruit—which I always had placed upon the table during dinner, because in my estimation it added to its dainty appearance—and then left us to ourselves, reappearing a few moments later with the coffee, which we always took together when dining alone. This she poured out and handed, together with the sugar bowl, on a dainty little tray. We never had milk served when we were by ourselves, as we prefer our coffee in its native simplicity, but of course when we had guests a jug of perfectly boiling milk was always added to the tray.

A month or so of this training soon turned raw

little Mary into a very creditable parlourmaid. Though she was naturally rather stupid, she was yet deft and low-voiced and soft-footed, so that she had everything in her favour, and although of course she occasionally made mistakes, I always corrected these as they arose, and very soon I had no need for correction.

The day after her arrival I put her through her paces as regarded the opening of the front door, showing in and announcing visitors, etc.

Here, too, she occasionally made very droll mistakes, but no matter how inclined I might be to do so, I never allowed myself to laugh at her, and in time she grew to be quite *au courant* with this part of her duties, and could discriminate between a man who wanted to sell us a patent brand of oats, and old influential friends of my husband's with the utmost nicety.

Her very worst and funniest mistake was when she was once—in obedience to my mandate that she must never, no never, bring anything to her master or mistress in her hands, but always place the article in question on a waiter before handing it—found endeavouring to balance the largest umbrella we possessed upon a tiny tray before taking it to my husband who was fuming and fretting in the hall, and in danger of losing his train to the City. Needless to say I had only had such articles as letters, cards, money, etc., in my mind when I had been giving her these particular instructions, but however she never repeated the offence.

I was very particular as to her dress. For

mornings she wore a gown of the darkest grey linen we could procure, with a broad turned down white collar. I never allow my servants to wear light prints for the very obvious reason that these increase the washing bills to no inconsiderable extent.

For afternoons she had, of course, the usual livery, black gown with white cuffs and collar, and a smart white apron. I think I have mentioned that I provided these latter myself.

Now on the face of it this may perhaps sound an extravagance, but I can assure my readers that it is not so in reality. Mary was only of average tallness, and therefore did not require very large aprons. Moreover, it would be manifestly impossible for her to purchase white aprons, etc., as well as clothe herself out of two shillings per week, which was all I could afford to pay her, so I found out a cheap little draper in the High Street, Kensington, who made a speciality of servants' aprons, etc., and got half-a-dozen or so at 8¾d. each, which were quite pretty enough to please the most fastidious. In addition to these I bought a single very smart one for which I paid 1s. 6¾d., for wear on our reception days, or when we had people to dinner, etc.

For the caps I only paid 2¾d. each. Of course at this price they did not boast "streamers," and though the latter were highly fashionable at that time, I made up my mind, not, I confess, without a pang, to forego them. "Half soiled cap strings," said I to myself, "are worse than no cap strings at all," and as I knew I could not afford to let Mary change them so frequently as she would otherwise have had to do, I resolved to let her do without them at all. As regards cuffs, except on very special occasions, we made shift with paper ones, because you can get six pairs of these for 1¾d., and really they look every whit as nice as their more costly brethren fashioned of linen. In addition to this I purchased a couple of smart aprons for cook, for such times as she should take her turn in attending to the door, or for when we had our little monthly receptions. Yes, ambitious as it may sound upon a housekeeping allowance of two pounds per week, I determined to have a reception, and moreover to have it all done properly. I knew that in my husband's profession, that of lawyer, the more people he knew the better it would be for him, and I made up my mind to get him on. " He *shall* get on," said I to myself, and as I knew well enough no one ever wants to visit people who are perpetually hard up, I also made up my mind that we never would be hard up, for of a surety no one who keeps within his income, be it even but a halfpenny to the good, can be said to be in this unpleasant predicament. To this end I, in a fashion, made friends with my cook; I tried to identify her interests with our own, and I am bound to say that I succeeded, although at the same time I was very careful never to let her overstep the boundary between mistress and maid, so that in a manner of speaking her familiarity never by any chance degenerated into contempt. How I managed this, however, I must tell you in another chapter.

CHAPTER V

THE SHOPS—HOW TO SELECT THEM

As soon as we were settled in West Kensington I made it my business to make a tour of the shops. To my surprise, however, I found them by no means as cheap as the comparatively low rents asked in the neighbourhood would have led me to suppose, and as out of two pounds per week I had to provide not alone food, but wine, ærated waters, and all the hundred and one daily expenses of a household, not to mention the laundry bill, in itself no inconsiderable item, I determined to go further afield. I tried the North End Road first, but though the shops there were exceedingly low in price, still the coster and barrow element prevailed to such an extent that I could not bring myself "to fancy" the things. Finally I tried Hammersmith and with the happiest result; the prices asked there being almost a half lower than in the ultra fashionable High Street, Kensington, and the quality—once I had learnt to carefully discriminate between what shops to go to and what to avoid—in no way below the average. The walk too from West Kensington to Hammersmith is by no means an unpleasant one, and 'bus and train are both available.

I found out first a good butcher, whose prices ran as follows :—

Beef, sirloin, 8d.

Rump Steak, 9d.
Beefsteaks, 8d.
Buttock steaks, 7d.
Silverside and back ribs, 6d.
Brisket, 4d.

Mutton was correspondingly moderate, whilst for New Zealand mutton of the " Canterbury Brand," the prices asked were :—

Shoulders, 5d.
Legs, 6d.
Loin, 4½d.
Neck, 4½d. and
Breast, 3d.,

the " River Plate Brand " being a fraction or so cheaper. Veal was also moderate in price. Pork I did not trouble about, as if you want good dairy-fed pork—and it is not safe to buy any other·—you must pay a fair price.

Having in my own mind suited myself with a butcher, I next went in search of a greengrocer and fruiterer, and found one close by, whose wares were of first-class quality and yet surprisingly cheap. " Thank goodness," thought I, " we shan't have to go without dessert " (we are both passionately fond of fruit), but here let me counsel my readers who may be tyros at housekeeping, never to buy fruit solely because it is cheap ; satisfy yourself that it is perfectly sound also, and if it isn't, let it severely alone, for it is as dangerous to buy unripe or over ripe fruit as it is to buy bad meat.

However, to go on.

My next move was in search of an egg shop, for on a housekeeping allowance of two pounds per week fresh eggs from the local dairyman at 2½d. apiece is an impossibility. At length I discovered one, whose prices varied from 16 to 20 a shilling, according to season; while fresh eggs were but a 1¼d. apiece. Now I wanted to give my husband thoroughly dainty cooking, and as really dainty cookery of the French *bourgeoise* sort is practically impossible without a plenitude of eggs, I determined to indulge in a shillingsworth every week, but first I had a little argument with myself.

"Suppose half of them should be bad," said I doubtfully. "It isn't likely they'll guarantee eggs at such a low price as that." Finally I hit upon the following plan. I gave the woman a "standing order" for one shillingsworth of the cooking eggs and three of the fresh ones, for all the year round, upon condition that she changed such as were tainted. At first she demurred, but when I pointed out that 1s. 3¾d. every week mounts up during a year to the respectable total of £3 8s. 8d., she agreed at once.

That difficulty over, I had to select my grocer and cheesemonger. This was easy, as King Street, Hammersmith, abounds in "Stores." Of these I selected the best, also as it happened, the largest, and then there only remained baker and dairyman to select.

Milk is the same price everywhere, so I decided to patronize a local man for that. As to bread I had visions of baking at home, but at present Penelope was unacquainted with the art, so finding that my stores sold what they termed "Farmhouse bread" at 2½d. per loaf, I bought a sample, and as it was "close," *i.e.* not spongy, and not unduly white—very white bread always contains a large proportion of alum, and is therefore indigestible in the extreme—I resolved to let the "Stores" supply me with this also. I have omitted to say that in all cases I arranged to have the things sent home, but I determined that I would have no calling for orders, as I consider this practice is the cause of half the dishonest cooks one hears of. You see it is not always possible or convenient for a mistress to go downstairs to the area door and give the orders herself, and if she does not do so small malpractices will creep in, and she has but little chance of either finding out or checking them.

Tired but hugely contented I was wending my way homewards, when I remembered that I had forgotten one of the most important items of all—the fishmonger.

Now my husband is extremely fond of fish, by way of preface to the more important part of the dinner, and as a bachelor he had always had it.

His income of £300 a year, though undeniably small for a married couple ranking as gentlepeople, and with the stern necessity of keeping up appearances ever before them, had been ample for a man in chambers, and as I knew he had been able to afford himself many little luxuries which he would now have to forego, it made me all the more anxious and determined that he should find no diminution, at least in his creature comforts.

Still fish is an article of food which is more or less dear, and I was puzzled to know just exactly how I

was going to squeeze a fishmonger's bill out of
that £2.

Suddenly a happy thought struck me. I remembered having seen in one of the best shops in
Kensington the following notice stuck up:—
" Contracts for fish daily, from 4d. per head," so
without loss of time I made my way to that identical
shop.

When I got inside I took my courage in both
hands, and boldly said I wanted enough fish sent
daily for at least three people, but did not wish to
pay more than three shillings per week, *i.e.* sixpence
daily.

"I don't at all mind the cheaper kinds of fish,"
added I hastily, seeing the salesman demur, "only
it must be *perfectly* fresh."

Greatly to my relief he assented to my proposi-
tion, and I am bound to say has carried his contract
out faithfully ever since.

Indeed, of quite the cheapest kinds of fish such, as
when in season, fresh herrings, hake, etc., we have
often had sufficient for six or seven people sent;
while now and again, even when salmon has been
dear, I have often had a dainty little cutlet, just
sufficient for two, arrive unexpectedly to my surprise
and delight.

When we have one of our modest dinner parties I
always, if they are in season, request fresh herrings
to be sent, since daintily fried or grilled and served
with well-made mustard sauce, few things are
nicer.

CHAPTER VI

HOW TO SPEND THE HOUSEKEEPING MONEY

WHEN I got home that morning I discovered that the few purchases I had made, simple as they were, had already produced an unconscionable hole in my week's allowance.

This alarmed me to no small extent, because I knew that no matter how much my husband might wish to do so, it was utterly out of his power to increase my housekeeping money by so much as a ten shilling piece. So, having taken my things off, I sat down and faced the situation boldly.

" There is nothing else for it," I said to myself resolutely. "If I am to succeed I must reduce this to a science."

Then the question presented itself, " How much can I actually allow for food ? " It was not easy to tell with the bugbear of a laundry bill ever before my eyes. But a happy thought struck me.

" Why not draw up a table of what you actually must send out, and keep to it, not exceeding it by so much as a pocket-handkerchief ? " Finally this is what I did, with the aid of the laundry price list. I append the list further on for the benefit of those readers who may wish to follow my example. I must tell you first, that I had already made a contract with the laundress to take the servants' washing at one shilling per head. I did this for two reasons. First and foremost because I wanted them always to look essentially smart, an impossibility this latter if they went about in home-laundried print gowns, caps, cuffs, collars, and aprons, for they had neither the experience to get them up properly, nor in a household such as mine the necessary time either; and secondly, because I did not—being perhaps ultra fastidious—quite like the idea of their under garments being washed together with my towels, serviettes, etc. This I felt pretty sure would be the case once my back was turned, and they were left to their own devices, and, as I had not the smallest intention of being for ever behind them, thus denying myself many small pleasures and outings, I decided on the course I have described.

The next serious item on the laundry bill was my husband's shirts, collars, etc. His underwear we washed at home, but I decided that he could not possibly do with less than a dozen collars per week, the extra ones I allowed in view of a probable evening engagement, three shirts, and a like number of pairs of cuffs he must have ; and then there was my own linen, that I decided would soon be ruined if trusted to the tender mercies of Penelope ; clean serviettes and tablecloths we must have, as these, too, would soon be completely spoilt, and a single sideboard cloth and five o'clock tea cloth to my mind came under the heading of absolute necessities. These I decided could go once a fortnight, and so, too, could the frilled pillow shams, the latter being articles which also call for the fostering care of a well-trained laundress. The d'oyleys I did not take into consideration, as being entirely of modern point, and needing no " getting up " in the ordinary sense of the word, I washed them out in the hand basin myself.

My toilet covers in all the rooms matched the curtains, being of plain bordered art linen in a shade of rather dark Japanese blue, and as they required no clear starching could be done at home quite as well as at the laundress', at about one-sixth of the cost. Pocket-handkerchiefs, towels, sheets, counterpanes, bed-spreads—the latter were also of the art linen—and household cloths of every description were also done at home, as were, of course, the socks and stockings. Finally, when arranged, my laundress bill stood as follows :—

GENTLEMAN'S.	s.	d.
Three shirts (at 4d. each)	1	0
One dozen collars (9d. a dozen)	0	9
Three pairs cuffs (1d. a pair)	0	3
And an occasional white waistcoat	0	6

My own washing, which was very moderate, as I was obliged, in plain language, to stint myself considerably, ran thus :—

LADIES'.		
Two pairs knickers (at 2d. a pair)*	0	4
Two chemises (at 2d. a pair)*	0	4
One nightdress	0	2
One white skirt, or a blouse sent occasionally	0	3
HOUSEHOLD.		
Three dinner cloths (at 3d. each)	0	9
One dozen serviettes (at 9d. a dozen)	0	9
Two pillow shams (or one sideboard and one tea cloth)...	0	2
Servants	2	0
Total	7	3

* NOTE.—Of course if combinations were worn in place of these the washing bill could be reduced by 6d. weekly.

When my husband did not send a white waistcoat I used to send a couple of washing blouses or some cuffs and collars of my own; at other times I slipped in my cuffs, etc., with the servants' washing, as the latter only wore linen cuffs occasionally, and the laundress had contracted to take anything they sent in reason for 1s. weekly.

The reader may, perhaps, think me unduly extravagant with the tablecloths and serviettes, but to this I would reply that the daintiest and most delicately cooked meal in the world will not *look* appetizing if served upon soiled table linen and accompanied by serviettes long past their pristine freshness, and as I have said before, I was determined that my husband should not, as the North Country folk say, " pig it " in any way. I knew that this would be rather difficult, nevertheless I set my wits to work determined to succeed, and that I did, I hope the following pages will show.

Having in my own mind disposed of the laundry bill to my complete satisfaction, I took out my little note-book and put down " Laundry, 7s. 3d."; and the fishmonger, with whom I had just concluded so satisfactory a bargain, coming to my remembrance, I followed it up with " Fishmonger, 3s." Then I recalled the egg merchant, and down went another entry of 1s. 3¾d. Next the baker suggested himself.

We were four people, all blessed with exceedingly healthy appetites, and there would be occasional callers at tea time to reckon in, so I did not see how we were to do with less than two loaves a day; at 2½d. a loaf that would mount up to 2s. 11d. So

down went "Bread, 2s. 11d." Bread naturally
recalled butter to my wandering imagination, and as
I had seen some excellent salt butter priced at
10d. a pound in a local butterman's, and a fresh
"Brittany" for 1s. 2d. per pound, I decided to
reserve for butter 1s. 10d. This allowed for half a
pound each for the servants, half a pound exclusively
for cooking, and half a pound of the aforesaid
Brittany butter for our two selves. We were not at
all fond of butter ourselves, except *in* the cooking,
so this amount was ample. Lard I did not allow
for, except in the shape of a very occasional odd
half pound, as I reckoned that the fat from the
soup, joints, etc., would, when clarified, provide us
with an ample frying medium.

I next bethought me of the stock pot, and for its
plenishment I put down "Bones, 6d.," and determined to give my butcher an order for the same
forthwith. With me to think is to act, so then and
there I sent off a post card desiring him to send me
6d. worth of beef and veal bones mixed every
Friday until further notice. Then I thought it was
about time to see how far I had got in my mental
spending, so I added the above items up, and they
totalled out as follows :—

				s.	d.
Washing ...	...	...	...	7	3
Fishmonger	...	...	...	3	0
Egg merchant	...	...	...	1	3¾
Baker ...	...	...	...	2	11
Butterman	...	...	...	1	10
Stock ...	...	...	...	0	6
	Total ...	...		16	9¾

35

This I found left me in hand with exactly £1 3s. 3d. less three farthings.

So I got my store list out and set to work. Of tea I decided we must have at least a pound, that would be just 1s.

Coffee we could not do without, since we were both so fond of it, and as unground coffee at 1s. 8d, and 1s. 10d. a pound was, alas! too expensive for us, I decided to try a " French mixture " at 1s. per tin, and when properly made we found it very excellent.

We both possess a sweet tooth, so for sugar I put down 6d., and this at 1½d. a lb. gave us a pound per head all round. A pound of cooking sugar was another 1½d., and half a pound of castor sugar at 2d. a lb. came to another 1d. ; total for sugar, 8½d.*

Then a whole host of absolutely necessary things came crowding in upon me. So finally I decided to take a pound of my own and stock a tiny cupboard which stood on one side of the kitchen as a store cupboard ; having come to this determination and remembering that the said cupboard would need replenishing, I put down the grocer's bill at 7s. weekly, allowing for soap, soda, blue, starch, wood, candles, matches, bath bricks, beeswax, turpentine, oil, hearthstone, blacking, blacklead, and all the hundred and one things needful in our laundry operations under that heading.

This left me with a surplus of just 16s. 2¼d. for the greengrocer, butcher, and florist combined, and,

* Sugar is liable to fluctuation. Since writing above it has advanced one farthing per pound.

I may as well confess it at once, how to divide this I really didn't know. However I resolved to make the experiment. So leaving the spaces opposite " Greengrocer " and " Butcher " vacant, I resolved to wait events and see what knowledge would be born of experience.

The next day was Saturday, and when in the due course of my shopping I reached the butcher's I noticed a fine large shoulder of New Zealand mutton hanging up, and upon enquiring I was told that if I liked to take it "entire" I could have it for 4½d. a pound ; it weighed just exactly 10 lbs. Needless to say I jumped at the offer, though first I took care to satisfy myself that the meat was perfectly sweet and in good condition.

This joint then cost me 3s. 9d.   How we treated it I must tell you later on.

I next journeyed to the greengrocer's, and here I ordered and paid for sixpennyworth of potatoes, at 5 lb. for 2d., which I reckoned should last us the week, a cauliflower of quite large size for 2d., two pounds of apples which I intended to use for dessert and which cost 2d. a pound, a 1d. lettuce, two pennyworth of onions, and a pennyworth each of carrots and turnips—these latter for the betterment of the soup—together with a large cabbage which cost me 1d.   Thus my greengrocer's bill came to exactly 1s. 6d., and this expenditure, with the dried beans, peas, etc., I already had in the house, I decided ought to be enough for some days.

CHAPTER VII

HOW I SHOPPED

WE were dining out that Saturday evening, so I was not troubled as to dinner, and I therefore decided that we would have the shoulder of mutton plainly roasted for the following day, and that the remains of a beefsteak pudding which we happened to have in the house would make a substantial supper for the two maids.

Now New Zealand mutton requires careful treatment and, accorded it, you will find that when properly roasted, if it has had its due meed of basting, it is in no way inferior to the ordinary English mutton, for which so many virtues are claimed. This is how I made Penelope treat ours.

First of all we cut off all the superfluous fat which was then reserved and afterwards melted down and clarified.

Next we placed the joint in the largest bowl we possessed, and just covered it with very hot, but not boiling water.

It was left in this bath for about a quarter of an hour, then taken out, dried thoroughly, dusted with a little flour, and roasted in the usual way, being plentifully basted every few minutes.

On Sunday we served it thus accompanied by red currant jelly, cauliflower and white sauce, and baked potatoes, cooked under the joint these latter. On Sunday evening a portion of it figured as a vinaigrette of mutton made as follows :—First I cut a sufficient number of slices from the lean part of the mutton to, as I calculated, serve for all our suppers. These were again cut into neat strips, dusted lightly with pepper and placed in a deep bowl. The lettuce before mentioned was carefully washed and dried until not a drop of moisture remained, then torn into pieces of a suitable size and added to the mutton, together with half-a-dozen cold waxy potatoes cut into slices, a little grated onion, salt to taste, and a couple of hard boiled eggs cut into quarters, the dressing being composed of oil and vinegar in the proportion of two table-spoonfuls of the former to one of the latter. It was then lightly but thoroughly mixed and served. We had prefaced it with a plateful of hot soup, and it was followed by a rice cream, of which I later append the recipe and a jelly, the latter made by using a 3½d. packet of table jelly, which produced a pint; home-made jellies, much as I should have liked to indulge in them, being beyond my means and Penelope's experience.

On Monday evening another portion of that mutton appeared at dinner as *mouton à l'Indienne*. Here is the recipe, if you wish to do likewise.

Take a penny packet of dessicated soup. Empty it into a basin and just cover it with a little water or stock and leave it to soak. Cut a sufficient number of slices from a cold roast shoulder of mutton, selecting if possible that part which is underdone. Place a bit of butter about the size of a walnut in a clean frying-pan, as soon as it melts add to it as much finely-chopped garlic as will go

39

on the point of a small knife, a large onion thinly sliced, fry for two or three minutes and then add the slices of mutton, and a large spoonful of Indian chutney. By this time the dessicated soup will have soaked up all the stock or water added to it ; add it to the meat, etc., together with a small cupful of either stock or water, cover the pan tightly, draw to the side of the fire, and simmer gently until the onions are quite cooked. Add salt and pepper to taste, boil up sharply for a few minutes in order that the gravy may reduce and thicken, and serve with a wall of mashed potato.

On Tuesday evening we had a dish of *croquettes de mouton,* which are made as follows :—

Take eight ounces of cold mutton, free it from skin and fat, and chop it finely. Then pass twice through the mincing machine, add to it sufficient bechamel sauce to make it of the consistency of very thick cream. Mix and spread the mixture on a large plate to the depth of about an inch. Leave in the larder until perfectly cold, then shape into balls about the size of a small tangerine; egg and bread-crumb these, and fry in boiling fat till of a light golden colour. Take out quickly, drain carefully, and serve with snow potatoes, handed separately. Here is an inexpensive recipe for the bechamel sauce mentioned above. Simmer half a pint of milk, with a bayleaf, a tiny blade of mace, a pinch of powdered sweet herbs, thyme, marjoram, etc., a small onion, a pinch of salt, and a few pepper-corns. As soon as the milk tastes strongly of herbs, remove the latter, knead an ounce of flour with an ounce of butter, and use it to thicken the milk, bring gently to the boil, rub through a fine gravy strainer or a hair sieve, and use as directed above.

On Wednesday evening the remains of our shoulder of mutton appeared in the guise of a curry, a dish of which my husband is very fond, and on the Thursday evening, the blade-bone, duly scored and rubbed with a devilling mixture, appeared as a savoury. The curry above referred to was made thus:—

Cut the remainder of the mutton, after freeing it from fat, into neat small squares. Place half an ounce of butter in a clean enamelled iron stewpan, when it oils add to it a large onion, sliced and finely chopped, a large apple, peeled, cored, and sliced, a dessertspoonful of dessicated cocoanut, and if liked, a small carrot, grated—the latter is unnecessary, but I consider it an improvement. Fry for two or three minutes, add a spoonful of curry powder and the mutton, and continue to fry for at least ten minutes, then add a little stock or water, sufficient to form the requisite gravy. Cover the pan tightly, draw it to the side of the fire, and simmer gently until the vegetables are thoroughly cooked. Add a spoonful of sifted sugar, a dessertspoonful of vinegar, and salt to suit your own taste. Boil up in order to reduce, and thicken the gravy, and serve garnished with a wall of rice in the ordinary manner. Very few English people boil rice properly. The correct method is this: After washing the rice thoroughly, it should be put on to boil in water, to which has been added a few drops of lemon juice and some salt. When quite tender, by which time the divisions in each grain of rice can be plainly seen, drain and then rinse twice in cold water, place in a cool oven until thoroughly dry, turning frequently with a fork, in order that it may be dry right through. If the above plan is followed you should have no cause for complaint that the rice is sticky or not properly cooked.

I will give you the recipes of our dinner during that week later on. For the present I will just say that we followed up that curry with an *entrée* of *chou à la crème*, as this, being particularly delicate and creamy, is very grateful to the palate after a spiced entree, such as curry. On Thursday I journeyed to the butcher's again. I have omitted to say that he also sold poultry, but he did, and my attention was attracted to a particularly large yellow fowl, which, though absolutely fresh and sweet, was only labelled 2s.

The knight of the cleaver explained the reason.

It was a soup, *i.e.* old fowl. " The very thing for a casserole," thought I. So I bought it, and bore it off in triumph, pausing at my greengrocer's to acquire a cauliflower, for which I paid 2d., and seven oranges which cost me 3d. Thus my expenditure that day was just under half-a-crown. When I got home, we treated that fowl thus : After being duly cleansed (I relegated the giblets to the stock pot, and reserved the liver for a savoury), we set to work to dress it *en casserole*.

Here is the recipe :

Place an ounce and a half of either clarified butter or dripping in a deep stewpan. As soon as it oils add the fowl, together with a split clove of garlic, a small blade of mace, a pinch of powdered sweet herbs, twenty peppercorns, or a quarter teaspoonful of pepper, a blade of mace, and, if possible, a couple of ounces of fat bacon, fry altogether until the fowl is of a bright golden colour all over, then draw the pan to the side of the fire, and let it continue to cook slowly for at least a couple of hours, basting it meanwhile every two or three minutes. At the end of the time, dish up the fowl on a very hot dish, remove all the herbs, etc., and drain off every particle of fat, dredge in a little flower to the gravy remaining, add to it the smallest possible amount of water, and salt to taste, stir it well up with the flat of a knife, bring to the boil, pour over the fowl, and serve with chipped potatoes. We followed it up with a vegetable *entrée*, cauliflower *au gratin*, and I think you would do well to do so also. I now had only eight odd shillings remaining out of my 16s. 2d., and Friday and Saturday's dinner had still to be provided, and in addition, Saturday's lunch, when, my husband, being at home, we always had a hot meat meal.

How I and the servants managed other days I must tell you later.

For Friday I provided a rump steak, which cost me just 1s. 6d., and weighed a trifle over a pound and a half. We grilled it, and served it with *maitre d'hotel* and straw potatoes, following it up with a dish of butter beans (they cost twopence a pound these latter), *à la Francaise*. The *maitre d'hotel* butter is made as follows: Take an ounce of butter and "work it" with a teaspoonful of minced parsley and half that quantity of chopped shallots, add to it a dash of pepper, fill a forcer with the mixture and pipe it on to the steak in two irregular lines right down the middle. If you haven't a "forcer," make two or three little conical bags, such as grocers sometimes put up pounds of sugar in, leaving a tiny hole open at the end. Fill the bag with the butter, and then squeeze through the small end on to the steak in the best patterns your genius can suggest.

For Saturday's lunch I bought eight New Zealand mutton kidneys, and served them *à la maître d'hotel* also, using for the purpose the remains of the butter made and left the night before, as I did not put it quite all on the steak. The kidneys were accompanied by some potatoes *lyonnaise*.

Here is the recipe :

Take some cold, and if possible waxy potatoes and cut them into slices about a quarter of an inch thick. Place half an ounce of butter on a clean frying-pan, and as soon as it melts add to it a very small onion thinly sliced, fry until the onion is thoroughly cooked, then add the potatoes and fry until very hot and slightly brown, dust with pepper, and if needed salt, then dish upon a hot dish and serve at once, sprinkle before serving with a little finely minced parsley.

By the way, I always kept parsley in the house. Buy a pennyworth every Saturday and keep it with the *roots only* in water ; by this means it will last the whole week round if the water is changed every day.

I had now a little over six shillings left, so

seeing some fine fat ptarmigan marked 10d. each, I bought one of these for our two selves and a little over half a pound of beef steak, which cost me 5d., for the two servants. The ptarmigan we had roasted plainly and served with a sweet gravy, made by adding a teaspoonful of red currant jelly—jam will do when jelly isn't obtainable—and a squeeze of lemon juice to the ordinary gravy, and then making the latter very hot, and an orange salad.

Here is the recipe for the latter :—

Wash a head of lettuce, and dry it thoroughly. Tear, *do not cut*, the leaves into pieces of a suitable size. Rub a clean *cold* salad bowl with a split clove of garlic. *Note.*—As it is absolutely impossible to make a successful salad in a bowl which is even in the slightest degree warm, the latter should never by any chance be kept in the kitchen or near any hot water pipes, etc. The coolest corner of the larder should be selected for its abode when not in use.

Place the lettuce in this and dust lightly with salt and pepper, then pour over it a couple of large tablespoonfuls of oil, and mix lightly, using your hands for the purpose. Add a little, a *very* little, grated onion, an orange, first peeled, and quartered, freed from skin and pips and cut up into small square pieces, and finally a tablespoonful of vinegar. Mix again, as lightly as possible, and serve at once. *Note.*—This salad should only be made immediately before it is required, unless you are able to keep it on ice, as otherwise it will be spoilt. And this rule I would remind the amateur at salad making holds good for all salads, but more especially those wherein, as in the case of the

45

foregoing recipe, fruit figures. The reason for this is obvious, as if allowed to stand, the juice from the fruit will " run " and render the salad heavy and practically uneatable.

Too much care cannot be directed towards drying the salad before adding the dressing. It is carelessness in this respect which is the cause of the lamentable failures sent up to table by so many English cooks under the misnomer of salad.

But to go on.

In addition to the ptarmigan, which of course came out of the previous week's housekeeping money, finding I had a small surplus in hand, I expended part of it on fruit, and then going the round of my little set of shops I " ordered in " for the following week. Having reached the butcher's I decided to invest in a joint of beef, and I got quite a large piece of back ribs, which, as I think I have mentioned before, is excellent for roasting though rather coarser in grain than the more costly joints such as wing ribs, sirloin, etc. This cost me just 3s. 6d., and weighed exactly 7 lbs. I reckoned that 5 lbs. would make quite a respectable joint for roasting purposes, so I requested the butcher to cut me off a piece weighing as nearly as possible two pounds, and this I determined to place in a marinade as soon as it arrived, and to braise it for the Monday's dinner. Then I went to the greengrocer's, and after purchasing some apples for a tart, some horse-radish—I was determined my husband shouldn't go without his favourite Russian sauce next day—and some bananas, which being just then particularly plentiful were to be had at the low price of a halfpenny each, and a cabbage, some onions, carrots, turnips, brussels sprouts and potatoes, my greengrocer's bill came to just 2s. all told.

I was wending my way to the Stores full of glee, when I suddenly remembered *I had forgotten the milkman's bill.* For a moment I felt inclined to burst out crying then and there in the street, but upon remembering that as I had just stocked my modest little store cupboard, and that therefore the grocer's bill would not come to more than four shillings at the outside, I took heart of grace. I had also been over liberal in my estimate of the bread we should require, for on some days I had only found it necessary to take a single loaf, so that altogether our bread bill for the week was only 2s. instead of the 2s. 11d. I had mentally set apart for it. Of milk we used a quart a day, taking a pint and a half in the mornings, and half a pint in the afternoons. So thus owing to the reduction in the grocer's bill, and to the extra elevenpence saved on the baker's bill, I was able to discharge my debt to the milkman, but the fright I had had taught me a lesson, and I determined to pay him every day. This I was easily able to do, as after a little time I found the household expenses vary, and by achieving various small economies, now and again when we had been out to dinner a good deal, in the butcher's and washing bills, and again in the greengrocer's and grocer's accounts, I was able to keep level with the milkman, although I have never quite been able to forgive myself for forgetting him in the first instance.

47

CHAPTER VIII

THE COOK—HOW TO TRAIN HER

As I have already told you before, I, in a sort of fashion, made a friend of my cook. When I commenced to train her, I began by, to a certain extent, taking her into my confidence, explaining pretty clearly that I was economical, not from choice, but from sternest necessity.

Most servants hate a *mean* mistress, but they will all respect a *careful* one, and so I took care to make mine understand, that while I did not intend nor desire to stint them, they must not waste even so much as a crumb while they were in my house. Fortunately for me the cook was naturally a good warm-hearted girl, and when I put things thus before her, she readily fell into my ways, and whenever a small economy of any sort was practicable, she was always eager to be the one to suggest it.

When first she entered my service her culinary accomplishments stood somewhat as follows. She could roast a joint very fairly, cook potatoes and the plainest kinds of greens, such as peas, beans, cabbages, etc. ; make a custard or pancakes and rice or tapioca puddings, and she also, so she said (I never tried her), could produce beef tea, mutton broth, etc.—fry fish after a fashion, and concoct one kind of tea cake. Her sauces were limited to a bread sauce of poultice-like consistency, and what she called white sauce.

She had never heard of French cookery. She did not know the meaning of stock, and frying in deep fat was to her as Greek.

Nevertheless she had a genuine liking for cooking, and so I determined to, by means of the utmost patience, turn her into a thoroughly good cook. This is how I set about it.

I explained to her, that where anything of a difficult nature was concerned, I would do it first before her, and then, giving her the recipe, should expect her to follow it out the next time without any assistance. "But," said I, "where anything fairly easy is in question, I shall expect you to manage without assistance from me. And bear in mind that if you attend to my instructions properly, *and go by the recipe*, you must be successful," I impressed upon her.

In addition to this, I wrote out all the recipes I gave her, myself, in a plain round hand, and in the simplest manner and language I could command. It is no use giving elaborately worded recipes to an inexperienced cook. It only confuses her, and serves no good purpose.

To this end I have often written and re-written my own recipes until I got them simple enough to suit me.

The second morning after my cook arrived, I commenced my instructions, having gauged her capabilities to my own satisfaction by the luncheon and dinner she had cooked the day before.

The bones for the stock had just arrived from

the butcher's when I made my appearance in the kitchen, and as at my request he had already chopped them into pieces of a suitable size they were quite ready for us to commence operations.

Here is the recipe for our stock :

Take a sufficient quantity of bones, sprinkle them liberally with salt, place on a clean dish, and then leave the dish in a hot oven for ten minutes. This browns the salt without cooking the meat left on the bones, and gives the soup a good colour. Next put the bones in a deep saucepan, and fill up with cold water. Place on the fire and bring gently to the boil. Then skim carefully. Add a *bouquet garni*—this consists of a bayleaf, a sprig of thyme and marjoram, and a sprig of parsley all tied together, a tiny blade of mace, twenty or thirty peppercorns, and half a dozen cloves and a little celery seed; don't add either carrots, turnips, or onions to the first boiling, as stock made thus turns sour far more quickly—half a cupful of cold water, and salt to taste. Draw the saucepan to the side of the fire, and let its contents simmer gently for six or seven hours. Every now and then you can remove the scum that will arise, but you must not allow the stock to cook quickly enough to reduce, or it will be spoilt. Next drain it off through a sieve into a deep soup bowl, and leave in the larder till next morning. By this time there will be a thick cake of fat floating on the top. Remove this and add to the fat pan to be clarified later.

Take care that not a particle of fat is left on the stock. Then take sufficient for your purpose, say about a quart. Place it in a clean saucepan, add to it a couple of very large onions peeled, sliced, and bring gently to the boil, simmer till the onions are quite cooked. Add salt if more is required, to suit your own taste, then serve at once. This is the French *Bouillon à l'Oignon.*

If you want a nice vegetable soup, add to a quart of the stock a couple of carrots scraped and thinly sliced, a couple of onions peeled and sliced—if obtainable leeks may be used in their stead—and a little previously boiled cabbage—the remains of a cold boiled cabbage will answer excellently for this purpose—and a few odd crusts of bread. When the vegetables are thoroughly cooked, you have *Croute au Pot.*

If you happen to have a few oddments of boiled beef that you can spare, add them to the above stock, and leave out the crusts, and you will have *Potage Bonne Femme.*

For a brown potato purée have ready a quart of this stock in a clean saucepan. Peel, wash, dry, and slice thinly, half a dozen large potatoes, and a couple of large onions. Place an ounce of clarified beef dripping in a clean frying-pan ; as soon as it melts put in the onions and potatoes and fry until they are of a nice dark brown colour, but take care that they do not burn. Then add them to the stock, draw the pan containing it to the side of the fire, let it simmer slowly until the vegetables are thoroughly cooked, then rub through a hair sieve. You must use the back of a wooden spoon to do this, and every now and again you must reverse the sieve and scrape the purée adhering to it into the bowl underneath. When you have got it all through return the purée thus obtained to a clean saucepan. Mix half an ounce of butter with half an ounce of flour to a smooth paste by means of a little cold stock or water; add this, which is called the *liaison*, to the purée, and stir briskly over a slow fire until your soup is quite smooth and creamy; then serve immediately and send fried crusts to table with it. I will tell you how to prepare these later.

American butter beans make a delicious purée. Take half a pound of them and boil them with an onion in a quart of stock until perfectly tender. Then rub them through a sieve in the same manner as the potatoes. Mix half an ounce of butter and flour with a little cold stock, and use this to smooth the purée; then serve as hot as possible. If you have no stock boil three-quarters of a pound of the beans in a quart of water, together with an onion stuck with a clove and a thick slice of carrot and turnip, and if you can get it, a bit of celery also. When the beans are quite tender, finish off the purée, just as you did the others, and serve as hot as possible. When chestnuts are cheap you can make a nice *chestnut purée* like this.

Boil fifty large chestnuts until you can peel them easily. Then scrape off the brown skin, put an ounce of butter into a clean stewpan, and when it melts add the chestnuts, an onion peeled and sliced, a tiny pinch of spice, a little pepper and salt, and a pinch of sifted sugar. Fry for five minutes, add a quart of water or stock, and simmer gently for three-quarters of an hour. Don't let the stock reduce. Then rub through a hair sieve, return to a clean saucepan, make very hot; add a little salt if required, and serve with fried crusts. You must give your stock a boiling up once a day if you wish it to keep sweet and fresh all the week round, and you must also wash the stock-pot out thoroughly each time it has been used, and then rinse it well with cold water. If you omit this precaution your soup will turn sour.

If you want macaroni or vermicelli soup, you have only to add a little of either to the above stock when it is boiling, and then continue boiling for a few minutes until the macaroni as vermicelli is cooked. You can buy a packet of Jullienne for fourpence at any grocer's. If you add a little of this to your stock you have Julienne soup.

We never had clear soup even when we had a dinner party, because this stock cannot be properly clarified without raw beef, and this adds to the expense, but if you wish for clear soup here is the recipe.

Take a quart of stock, add to it four ounces of raw minced beef, the whites and shells of two eggs, a bit of celery, and a shalot; bring to the boil, stirring carefully every few minutes. Then simmer gently for an hour and a half; strain through a soup serviette, and serve at once. You can add a little sherry to this soup if you like, and you can garnish it with a few squares of boiled savoury custard, or a little Julienne, in fact, anything you please. But it is not a strictly economical soup, and therefore I do not recommend it, as even the small quantity of beef necessary to clarify it adds to the expense.

When you have a dinner party do as we did, and serve a well-made purée, and you will find that most

53

people appreciate it, because it is a thing they don't get every day, whereas clear soup is a standing dish at every dinner-party one goes to.

When white artichokes are in season and cheap, you can get them at two pounds for 1½d. Purée of artichokes is as nice a thick soup as it is possible to make.

Here is the recipe :

Peel and slice three pounds of artichokes, and two large onions. Put an ounce of butter into a clean stewpan, when it melts add the onion with a suspicion of nutmeg, a little pepper and salt, and a couple of lumps of sugar. Fry for two or three minutes, but don't let the onions acquire any colour. Then add the artichokes and a quart of either milk, water, or stock, simmer for an hour and a quarter, then rub through a hair sieve, and return to a clean saucepan. Make very hot and serve with fried crusts. When you want to be very extravagant a pennyworth or twopennyworth of cream added to this soup will be found a great improvement, but it is by no means necessary.

If you want to make lentil soup you need only follow the recipe given for the butter bean purée, and you can made a delicious purée of green peas by using the pods only.

This is the method :

Wash and string all the best pods from half a peck of peas, rejecting those which have a yellow tinge. Place an ounce of clarified beef dripping in a stewpan, add to it a large onion peeled and thinly sliced, a good-sized sprig of mint, and the pea pods, fry for ten minutes but don't let them burn. Then

54

add a quart of water and simmer very slowly until the vegetables are thoroughly cooked. Rub through a hair sieve, returning the pureé thus obtained to a clean saucepan, knead an ounce of flour with an ounce of butter and then mix it to a smooth paste with a little milk. Add this to the pureé, and stir slowly until it becomes perfectly smooth, add salt, pepper, and sifted sugar to taste. Make very hot and serve with fried crusts. A leaf or two of spinach added to the pods, etc., when cooking will give this soup a rather brighter colour, but do no. use the so-called "vegetable colourings" which are sold, as these, besides adding to the expense often contain arsenic and are therefore to be avoided.

If you want a brown onion soup fry half a dozen very large onions in an ounce of clarified beef dripping until they are a good deep colour, but do not allow them to burn. Then add them to a quart of your stock. Draw the pan to the side of the fire and let the contents simmer slowly until thoroughly cooked.

Next rub through a hair sieve and return to a clean saucepan, mix half an ounce of flour with half an ounce of butter and make to a paste with a little cold stock, then add to the soup and stir until it becomes smooth and creamy. Add salt and pepper to taste, and if it is at all pale in colour a few drops of soy, or Parisian essence. Make very hot and serve with fried crusts handed separately.

Carrot soup may be made in the same way. Fry the carrots together with an onion for at least ten minutes after slicing them thinly, and then finish according to the above recipe. A little sugar is an improvement to a purée of carrots, which is generally called *Potage a la Crecy*.

When turnips are cheap, you can make a delightful purée of turnips by following the recipe for purée of artichokes. Parsnips, too, make a very good purée. Add a little sugar to both of these, but do not allow the vegetables to acquire any colour whatever.

You must not think, however, that I confined my instructions to cook, solely to soups.

Far from it.

As soon as I had shown her how to make stocks, I proceeded to put her through her paces as regards the fish, which as I think I have already told you we had sent in every day.

She had little or no idea of frying this properly, and a " bath of fat " was a thing she had never even heard of, so as a step in the right direction I taught her first how to utilize and clarify the dripping from the joints and soup. When we had collected a sufficiency of this (we reserved a large bowl for its sole reception), we proceeded to clarify it.

Here is the recipe :

Pour over the bowl containing the fat to be clarified enough boiling water to nearly fill it. Then leave in the larder till perfectly cold. When cold the cake of fat will be found floating on top. If it is very dirty—*i.e.*, full of small brown specks—repeat the above process again, and if necessary twice. The fat is then fit for use. The bottom of the cake may be lightly scraped in case any impurity still remains.

But to go on.

The fish our fishmonger mostly sent us varied from slip soles and salmon, turbot, cod, halibut, and mackerel down to hake and fresh herrings.

This is the recipe for frying fish in deep fat. Fill a perfectly clean saucepan three parts full of clarified fat, and then bring it to the boil. *Note.*—Fat has not reached the boiling point until it is perfectly still, by which time a faint blue smoke will be seen rising from it. As soon as this appears put in the article to be fried *at once*.

Supposing, for instance, you wish to fry a pair of soles, wash and dry, and then egg and bread crumb them in the usual manner. Plunge them into the boiling fat and fry till of a light golden brown hue. Take out quickly, drain carefully and send to table at once, accompanied by whatever sauce is to be served with them. To egg fish economically use a small brush. These cost three-pence each, and can be bought at any ironmonger's or at the Stores. You should keep two, one for meat and pastry, and one for fish, and they must be washed, and put to dry on the top of the stove plate rack as soon as you have finished with them.

If these brushes are used when egging instead of the old fashioned wasteful mode of slapping the article to be cooked into the beaten egg, a single egg will suffice for both fish, and, say, a dish of cutlets. When beaten up, divide the egg equally and place a half in a couple of saucers. Use, and then bread crumb the article in the usual way.

When a piece of cod or halibut or turbot was sent we generally indulged in coquilles for dinner.

These are made as follows :

57

Boil half a pound of any kind of white fish in the usual manner. When quite done—it must not be *over* done—skin and bone it, and separate it lightly into large flakes; you must use a fork for this. Have ready half a pint of well flavoured bechamel sauce, add the flaked fish to this, and make very hot; you must toss lightly to avoid burning. Have ready four or five scallop shells and fill them with the mixture, scatter fried bread crumbs on top, place in a hot oven for from five to ten minutes and serve at once. *Note.*—When you have only a small piece of fish, and wish to provide for a larger number of people than the above, a little previously cooked macaroni cut · into short lengths may be added to the fish, etc., with advantage, and if cheese is not to appear in any of the other dishes, a little may be grated on to the top of each of the coquilles, and will be found a vast improvement. The coquilles should in any case be of a light golden hue on top, when taken from the oven, but quite soft underneath.

Here is the recipe for the sauce :

Place half a pint of milk in a clean white saucepan. Add to it a small onion stuck with a clove, a tiny blade of mace, half-a-dozen peppercorns, just a grate of nutmeg, a pinch of sweet herbs (or else a tiny sprig of thyme or marjoram), and a bayleaf and a small sprig of parsley. Simmer slowly together until the milk is well impregnated with the herbs, but don't let it reduce, *i.e.* boil away. Then strain into another saucepan, and thicken with an ounce of flour and an ounce of butter kneaded together. Stir gently over a slow fire till of the consistency of very thick cream, when use as directed.

Sometimes we treated our piece of cod or halibut, as the case might be, a little differently and served it *au fromage*. Here is the recipe. Place half a pint of milk in a clean saucepan, wash and wipe the fish perfectly dry and rub it over with a split onion, salt the milk to taste, and then add the fish and simmer slowly until thoroughly cooked. *Note.*—Don't let it over cook. Take it out and dish up on a hot dish, thicken the milk in which it was cooked with a bit of butter and little flour kneaded together, about half an ounce of each. When it is of the consistency of thick cream add to it a couple of ounces of grated cheese, and stir until the latter is thoroughly melted. Make hot, pour over and around the fish and serve at once. If you do not like cheese, leave out the latter, and in its stead add a few drops of lemon juice, and a little finely minced parsley. If you happen to have any cold floury potatoes left, treat them like this and make a dainty wall of them round the fish. Rub half a dozen large cold potatoes through a fine wire sieve. Place them in a clean saucepan with a bit of butter about the size of a walnut, a dash of pepper, salt if needed, and a gill of hot milk. Beat up as lightly as possible, using a silver fork for the purpose, and when very hot use as directed above. The remains of a dish of cold boiled white artichokes is excellent if used in this way, and either potatoes or artichokes will be found to eke out a small portion of fish very successfully, if unexpected guests, etc., arrive.

E   59

CHAPTER IX

THE COOK—HOW TO TRAIN HER (*continued*)

ANOTHER inexpensive way of treating a small piece of boiled or raw white fish is as follows :—

Cream of fish.   Rub half a pound of either raw or boiled fish through a fine wire sieve, add to it a teacupful of well-cooked rice, the chopped whites and yokes of two hard boiled eggs, and a little less than half a pint of white sauce made as directed for the coquilles of fish in the foregoing chapter.   Add the well-beaten yoke of one egg and the whites of two whisked to a froth.   Mix lightly.   Grease a plain mould thoroughly, fill it with the above mixture, tie down tightly with a well greased paper and steam for an hour and a quarter.   Add a teaspoonful of essence of anchovy, or else a dessertspoonful of Harvey sauce to a gill and a half of white sauce.   Make very hot, slip the cream of fish out on to a hot dish, pour the sauce over and around it, and serve immediately.

If you do not possess a steamer you can utilize an ordinary saucepan in the following manner :—

Place a cheese plate upside down in a saucepan. Pour boiling water round it to the depth of say two and a a half inches, place the mould containing the fish or whatever the article in question may be on top of the inverted plate, draw the pan to the side of the fire and cook for the requisite time.   *Note.*—

The water must not be allowed to stop boiling, and if it reduces, add more boiling water to make up the deficiency.

When we had mackerel we treated it as follows :

Split and clean the mackerel and reserve the soft roes to serve as a savoury, then wipe each fish over lightly with a bit of greased paper. Having done this, wipe the bars of the gridiron with the same paper. Dust each fish lightly with a little pepper, and then grill on both sides. The only requisite for grilling properly is a perfectly clear fire. Make it up with cinders early in the afternoon, say about four. Leave the dampers out, and by dinner time you should have an exquisitely clear red fire.

When the fish are quite cooked, place a little *maitre d'hotel* butter in the centre of each and serve at once. Fresh herrings are excellent if treated in the same way. When a small piece of salmon arrived, as small pieces of this fish do not boil well, we used to proceed thus :—

Wipe the salmon over lightly with the corner of a clean cloth, on which has been squeezed the juice of half a lemon. Then wrap it up in a piece of clean, well greased white paper, and bake in a moderate oven. Serve with *Dutch sauce*. Take a gill of hot white sauce, add to it the well beaten yolk of an egg, a teaspoonful of finely minced parsley, and a few drops of lemon juice. Make very hot, but don't let it boil or it will curdle and be spoilt. This sauce is greatly improved by the addition of a tablespoonful of cream, and you can serve it with either salmon, turbot, halibut, or cod which has been cooked in the manner just described for salmon.

A curry made from cod is very good. Follow the recipe given for a curry of cold mutton. It will form an excellent fish course for a cold winter night.

Whiting are best fried and served with Dutch or anchovy sauce. The latter is made by adding a teaspoonful or more according to the quantity of anchovy sauce to some white sauce. A couple of drops of lemon juice are considered an improvement by some cooks.

A fish pie is a good luncheon dish. We often used to have it for lunch when we were going out to dinner in the evening and wanted to utilize the daily portion of fish, and there was generally enough of the pie left for the servants supper also. Here is the recipe:

Fish Pie:—Take from half a pound to three-quarters of a pound of any white, cooked fish. Free it from skin and bone. Flake it carefully. Have ready four ounces of cooked macaroni, cut it into short lengths, and add it to the fish. Mix lightly. Have ready also half a pint of bechamel sauce, add to the fish, etc., and mix again. Fill a pie dish with the mixture and cut up a couple of hard boiled eggs on top. Mash half a pound or more of either freshly boiled or cold boiled potatoes with a little warm milk and a bit of butter. Cover the whole with the potato paste. Scatter bread crumbs on top, and place a few bits of butter here and there. Bake for half an hour in a moderate oven, and then serve as quickly as possible.

You will find the recipe for bechamel sauce earlier in the book. *Note.*—Do not attempt to make this pie with any brown fish, such as mackerel, herrings, etc. Smoked haddock, however, is excellent when fresh fish is unobtainable. Note also that the soft roes of the above fish should never be cooked with them. Always take them out as they make most excellent savouries.

You must not think that I taught cook all these fish dishes at once. The plan I followed was this. I used to give her, as soon as she got on a little, and was to be trusted alone, two fresh recipes every day. For example. A new soup, and say a new *entrée*; or a new fish dish and a new pudding. (Savouries I did not count, as these are most of them so easy.) Thus I felt sure I was not overloading her intelligence in any way, and I would advise my readers to follow out this rule for themselves, as by so doing, they will avoid confusing an inexperienced girl, and also the mistakes and waste which are bound to result if she is confused.

Another thing I was very particular to do was to exercise great patience. Believe me, *you cannot* train a cook without it.

Encourage her, too, to ask questions, and tell her the why and wherefore of everything.

Many girls who know but little of cookery are apt to be very careless as to cleanliness. I do not mean cleanliness in the ordinary sense of the word, but such things as this.

They will go straight from handling fish or meat to make a pudding or mix a salad, without dreaming that they are guilty of gross carelessness. To avoid this, always reserve a bowl full of water close at hand during the time cooking operations are on, and insist on your cook washing her hands as need arises.

Needless to say the bowl should be kept solely for this purpose, and should not be used for anything else.

You will find that after a little drilling in this respect it will gradually grow into a habit, and you will not have to dread your cutlets coming to table with a decidedly " fishy " flavour about them, nor your afternoon tea cakes making their appearance to all outward seeming perfectly right, but tasting strongly of that at once, best and worst of all vegetables, the onion.

Here are some of the recipes which my little cook rapidly acquired.

Mutton cutlets *à la Firval*.

Boil six large onions and a couple of pounds of potatoes until quite cooked, then drain carefully, and rub both through a fine wire sieve. Flavour with salt and pepper, and the tiniest possible pinch of spice. Mix into a stiffish purée with a little warm milk, then make very hot in a saucepan and pile up lightly in the middle of an entrée dish. Arrange half a dozen or more fried mutton cutlets round and serve at once. The cutlets must be egged, bread crumbed, and fried in deep fat, till of a golden brown, then take out quickly, drain carefully, and use as directed.

New Zealand neck of mutton produces excellent cutlets.

Buy the whole neck. Then you can have a portion of it roasted or braised one day, and the remainder treated as above on the following or the day but one after, while the scrag will make an excellent fresh stew. Mutton, you must remember, is all the better for being well hung in a cool and dry larder. You can braise the mutton as follows :—

Braised mutton *à la Provençale.*

Take from two to four pounds of neck of mutton and trim it free from skin and superfluous fat. Place an ounce and a half of clarified beef dripping in a clean deep stewpan, and as soon as it melts add the mutton and a finely chopped clove of garlic, and fry till of a light brown colour. Turn the meat frequently to ensure its being of an equally good colour all over. Then add to it a couple of turnips peeled, sliced and cut into tiny square pieces, a couple of carrots, scraped and sliced, and if obtainable, a little chopped celery. Continue to fry for ten or fifteen minutes, then just cover the meat with stock—failing this water can be used— add half a dozen small onions, cover the pan tightly, draw it to one side of the fire, and let it simmer slowly until the contents are thoroughly cooked. This should take about three hours. Every now and then you must take off the lid and remove all the scum, grease, etc. As soon as the vegetables are thoroughly tender, dish up the meat on a hot dish, garnish with the vegetables, and place it in the oven to glaze. This will take about ten minutes. Meanwhile pour away all grease from the liqour in which it was cooked, and thicken the gravy remaining with half an ounce of flour, and half an ounce of butter kneaded together. Make very hot, pour over and around the meat and vegetables, and serve, accompanied by roast potatoes. Beef, either filet, back ribs, or silverside, is delicious if cooked after the foregoing manner. The turnips should be omitted and double the quantity of carrots and onions used in their stead.

Note.—The clove of garlic must be removed if it has been put in whole, but personally I prefer it finely chopped, though I am quite willing to admit that this may not appeal to English tastes.

If liked a dish of dressed macaroni may be served with either beef or mutton cooked in this mode.

As soon as cook could braise properly we went on to blanquettes. Now even the cheapest parts of veal make a delicious blanquette if treated aright. The great thing, of course, is not to overdo the flavouring, for the rest a blanquette may be said to principally cook itself.

Here is the recipe :

Take from three to four pounds of veal, neck or cushion, it does not matter which. Place an ounce of butter in a perfectly clean stewpan. As soon as it oils add the veal, and fry for ten minutes, but take care that the meat does not acquire even the faintest particle of colour, as this would quite spoil the appearance of the dish. Next take out the veal, and place it in a clean stewpan, add to it a large onion stuck with a clove, a bayleaf, and a small blade of mace. Add also enough milk to just cover the meat, then draw the pan to the side of the fire, cover tightly, and simmer gently until the meat is thoroughly done. This will take from two to two

66

hours and a-half, and care must be taken that the milk does not reduce ; should it do so more must be added.

When quite cooked dish up the veal on a hot dish, thicken the milk remaining in the saucepan with an ounce of flour and an ounce of butter kneaded together (first removing the onion, clove, mace, etc.), stir till the sauce is of the consistency of thick cream, make very hot and serve, accompanied by a dish of dressed macaroni. When mushrooms are cheap, four ounces of these cleaned and finely chopped may be added to the blanquette with great advantage, but if not obtainable, a dozen button onions gently stewed in the milk, may take their place, and are also a great improvement.

An old fowl stewed in the foregoing fashion, if allowed plenty of time in which to cook, will be found so tender as to be very little inferior to spring chicken.

In this case the milk should not quite cover it, but it must be frequently basted. Rabbits may also be prepared in this fashion, and will be found much more delicate than when cooked in the ordinary way.

The dressed macaroni before referred to is prepared as follows :—

Throw half a pound of macaroni into a saucepanful of absolutely boiling water, add a dessertspoonful of salt, and cook quickly until quite tender, by which time it should have absorbed the best part of the water. Then drain carefully. Place half an ounce of butter in a clean enamelled iron saucepan, as soon as it melts add the macaroni and toss for two or three minutes. Then add two or three ounces of grated cheese and continue to toss until the cheese has melted and become quite stringy. Dish up on a very hot dish and serve as quickly as possible. Spaghetti, which is a smaller make of macaroni, is also delicious if dressed after this fashion, and I have even known vermicelli treated thus with the happiest possible results. But bear in mind that neither macaroni, spaghetti or vermicelli will bear over-cooking with equanimity.

Another inexpensive *entrée*, greatly beloved of men, is known as *Tournedos aux Anchois*. It is made thus :

Take a pound of either beef or rump steak, rub it over with a split clove of garlic, and then lightly brush it with oil. Cut into neat strips, say four or five to the pound. Dust these with pepper, and then grill them over a clear fire. While they are grilling, work half an ounce of butter with a teaspoonful of anchovy paste—failing the paste you can use a few drops of essence of anchovy instead,—and a little finely minced parsley; pipe a little of this on to each steak, and send to table immediately accompanied by fried potatoes, or potato or artichoke chips.

Beef olives are by no means expensive. We always make ours like this :

Take a pound of very thinly-cut beef-steak, and cut it into pieces of a suitable size, rub each of these with a clove of garlic, and then place a thin strip of larding bacon upon each. Make a farce as follows :—Two tablespoonfuls of bread crumbs, a bit of butter the size of a walnut, pepper and salt to taste, and a teaspoonful of finely-minced parsley. Bind with the yoke of an egg, place a little upon each of the olives, then roll and secure with clean white cotton, or else make half a dozen tiny skewers from a stick of firewood, and use these instead. Place an ounce of clarified beef dripping or butter in a clean stewpan, and as soon as it melts add the olives and a sliced onion, and fry for ten minutes, then add a gill or more of either stock or water, draw the pan to the side of the fire, and let its contents simmer slowly until thoroughly cooked. The time this will take depends to a great extent upon whether the steak is tough or tender. The coarser kinds of steaks, such as buttock, taking twice as long as beef or rump steak would do.

When cooked, dish up the olives on a hot dish and place in the oven. Thicken the gravy remaining with a little flour and a bit of butter kneaded together, add a few drops of Parisian essence or China soy—to make the gravy of a good colour— and the peel from two or three finely-minced olives.

Boil up sharply, pour over the meat and serve.

Beef kidney is delicious stewed in the same way, but instead of stuffing this, you must cut it up into small neat pieces and roll the larding bacon, and stuff that with the force meat. In all other respects the recipe is the same.

Another nice *entrée* of beef is—

Bœuf aux Crevettes. Take a pound and a half of beef, or buttock steak. Mix a dessertspoonful of oil with a teaspoonful of vinegar, add to it a pinch of sweet herbs, a dust of pepper, a slice of onion, and a bit of lemon peel. Mix and then place the steak in this, leaving it for half-an-hour, then turn over, and let the other side soak for half-an-hour also.

Take out and wipe dry.

Place half an ounce of butter or beef dripping in a clean stewpan, when it melts add the steak and a couple of finely-minced shalots, and fry for ten or twelve minutes. Next add a gill and a half of either stock or gravy, cover the pan tightly, draw it to the side of the fire and simmer slowly for an hour and a half, take out the steak and dish it up on a hot dish. Thicken the gravy in which it was cooked with a little flour and a bit of butter about the size of a walnut. Stir till it gets smooth and creamy, then add a little finely-grated lemon-peel and twopenny-worth of picked shrimps. If the gravy is not a good colour a few drops of China soy may be added also.

Make hot, pour over the steak and send to table.

If you leave out the shrimps and add a couple of pickled walnuts instead, you have *stewed steak à la Française*. And if you use a tablespoonful of Chutney instead of the walnuts, you will have *steak à la Indienne*.

These two last-named should be served with a dish of boiled lentils instead of potatoes. When cooked toss the lentils in a little bit of butter, and add a dust of pepper and just a squeeze of lemon juice before sending to table. Buy the red and not the green variety of lentils, as the latter take much longer soaking and require more time when cooking than the other smaller kind. A braised roll of beef served with a soubise sauce makes a delicious dinner dish, and one, moreover, quite good enough for a little dinner party. Buy a piece of silverside, weighing about five pounds. This, if American beef, will cost you 6d. a pound—2s. 6d. for the joint. Wipe it quite dry, and place in a marinade, made like that described for the beef steak. Leave it in this for at least two hours, then take out and wipe till perfectly dry. Place an ounce of clarified beef dripping in a clean deep stewpan; when it melts add the beef, together with a bay leaf, and a liberal dust of pepper, a carrot, a turnip, and a large onion. Fry for fifteen minutes; then add sufficient stock to cover the meat, put the lid on tightly, draw the pan to the side of the fire, and simmer slowly for two hours and a half. Every now and then you must remove the scum which will rise to the top, but do not allow the stock to reduce or to reach boiling point, or the joint will toughen and be spoilt. While the beef is cooking prepare the following sauce:—Simmer three large onions in a little better than half a pint of milk until thoroughly tender, then take out and pass through a fine sieve, together with a floury potato. Return to the milk and mix well together. Mix a tablespoonful of flour to a paste with a little cold milk, and use to thicken the purée; season highly with salt, pepper, and a little grated nutmeg; then add bit by bit half an ounce of butter, and make very hot. By this time the meat will be cooked; take it out of the stock, drain carefully, and place in the oven to glaze brightly. This will take about ten or fifteen minutes. Pour the sauce around it and send to table at once. Duchess or fried potatoes should accompany this dish. *Note.*—Soubise sauce when properly made should be rather thicker than double cream.

The liquor in which the beef was braised should be poured through a strainer into a clean bowl, and placed in the larder till next day. Then remove the cake of fat floating on the top, and save the stock for gravy, or else add it to the soup bowl.

A delicious sauce for serving with a piece of beef braised in the foregoing fashion can be made like this :—Make half a pint of ordinary white sauce, then add to it a spoonful of finely-grated horse radish, a teaspoonful of sugar, half a teaspoonful of made mustard, and a squeeze of lemon juice ; make very hot, and send to table immediately. This is known as *Sauce Russe*, and it may be served with either roast or boiled, as well as braised beef, but is not suitable for white meats.

Occasionally I invested in a pound or so of beef steak, or fresh beef pieces, and we had a beef steak pudding. When making this, always add an onion, it will be found a great improvement ; the crust should have an egg or a couple of eggs mixed in with the dough, as this lightens and altogether improves the latter. Any scraps of cold beef which may be left from a joint should never be wasted. Free them from fat, pass through the mincing machine, and turn into Croquette de Bœuf. The recipe is the same as that given for Croquettes de Mouton, in a previous chapter.

If croquettes have already appeared once in the week, try a savoury mince served with poached egg on top and fried croutons in place of the old-fashioned sippets of toast.

Make the mince like this:—

Pass the meat through a mincing machine, place half an ounce of butter in a clean pan; when it oils, add a finely-minced shalot and a little parsley, and fry for two or three minutes; then add the minced beef, together with a teaspoonful of catsup and a gill or more of stock, according to the quantity of meat; season with pepper and salt, and a little grated lemon peel. Stir slowly until the stock is nearly all absorbed, then dish up, garnish with poached eggs and fried croutons, and serve. Very few plain cooks know how to fry properly, but if care is taken the operation is really a very easy one.

To fry croutons. Fill the saucepan half full of clarified fat. As soon as it ceases to bubble and a thin blue smoke begins to rise, throw in the croutons and fry till of a light brown. Take out quickly, drain carefully, and use at once. For the croutons themselves, cut slices about a quarter of an inch thick, from a stale loaf. For " finger croutons " cut these into long strips. For garnishing cut into squares about two inches and a half each way. For soup, cut into small diamonds. For savouries, stamp out into fancy rounds, with the aid of a pastry cutter. For sweets, cut out into fancy rounds of a larger size. Fry any or all of these in the manner described above and use at once.

73

Croutons should never stand in the oven or they will spoil.

To fry potatoes. First peel and wash them in the ordinary way; then cut into slices about half as thick as a shilling, wash and dry these thoroughly. Have a saucepan half full of boiling fat. Throw in the potatoes, a few at a time, and fry till of a light golden brown colour. Take out quickly, drain carefully, sprinkle with a little salt, and serve immediately.

Artichoke chips are delicious with either grilled or braised steaks. Peel and slice the artichokes to about the thickness of a shilling; wash and dry them carefully, and then fry as described for potatoes.

You must bear in mind that neither potatoes nor artichokes will fry properly if they are put into the fat while they are still damp. They must be *thoroughly* dried, or they are certain to be spoilt. Also you must never put in too many at one time (and this holds good for every kind of article to be fried), or else the fat will be chilled, and the potatoes, artichokes, croquettes, or whatever it is will be soddened and completely spoilt.

You must never leave the fat to get cold in the saucepan when you have finished frying. Always empty it out through a clean gravy strainer into a clean bowl, and place the latter in a cool corner in the larder till next required. If you have several things to fry, you can use the same fat right through by proceeding thus.

Fry the fish, strain the fat carefully through a clean strainer into another saucepan, bring to the boil again and cook your dish of cutlets. Strain again, bring once more to the boil, cook your croutons for the vegetable entrée or sweet or savoury, and then repeat the straining process, and put the fat back in the larder in its accustomed place, and I can assure you if you have strained the fat carefully, and brought it each time up to boiling, *i.e.* the blue smoke point, you need have no fear that any of the articles of diet cooked will savour of their predecessors in that fat.

Another point of importance in frying is not to *over* fry. As a general rule, fish, cutlets, croutons, etc., should be of a bright golden brown in hue, whilst potatoes, or artichoke chips, etc., should be of a bright yellow gold colour if cooked to perfection.

By noting this, and following the above simple rules, anyone should be able to fry quite as successfully as an experienced cook.

Note.—Shake the saucepan occasionally when frying, this will prevent the potatoes or whatever the article in question may be, from sticking to the bottom and burning.

The above is known as frying in deep fat, and it is not only more economical than the ordinary method beloved of English cooks, but food cooked in this way has always a far daintier appearance than that which has been subjected to the ordeal of an ordinary frying-pan.

F

CHAPTER X

OCCASIONALLY, as cook grew more and more experienced, we indulged in rather more elaborate entrées. That is of course, when funds permitted, or as I had been able to save in other directions.

When lamb's sweetbreads were cheap we often indulged in a *fricassée*. Here is the recipe :

Take a shillingsworth of lamb's sweetbreads. Place them in a clean bowl, and pour over them a jugful of perfectly boiling water. Repeat this twice. Then take out, drain carefully, and reserve on a plate till needed. Place an ounce of butter or clarified beef dripping in a clean stewpan. When it oils add to it a carrot, peeled, and cut into tiny squares. A large onion peeled and finely chopped, a little minced parsley, a dust of pepper and salt, and a little grated lemon peel.

Fry for a couple of minutes, add the sweetbreads, and continue to fry for another ten minutes. Then add half a pound of flageolets—these cost sixpence a pound, and are in season at the same time as the sweetbreads—which have been soaked for a couple of hours in cold water. Add sufficient stock or water to just cover, and simmer gently until the vegetables are thoroughly cooked. Thicken with a little flour and a tiny bit of butter, add salt and pepper to taste, and a few drops of colouring. Make very hot and serve with roast or boiled potatoes. Sometimes we indulged in a dish of *Vols au vent*, and for these, as my cook could not make creditable puff pastry, we used to buy half a dozen penny patty cases. Any confectioner will supply these. Here is the recipe for the *Vols au vent*.

Take sixpennyworth of lambs' sweetbreads, and blanch them as described above. Then drain them and place in a clean saucepan with half a pint of milk, a bay leaf, and a small onion. Simmer slowly till cooked, but don't let the milk reduce. Take out the bay leaf, sweetbreads, and onion. Thicken the milk with an ounce of flour and an ounce of butter kneaded together, add pepper and salt to taste, and a tiny grate of nutmeg. Cut the sweetbreads into small neat squares. Return them to the sauce. Make very hot. Fill the patty cases with the mixture. Place them in a very quick oven for ten minutes, and serve at once. *Noisettes de Veau au Tomates* is another delightful little entreé for a *diner a deux*. Buy half a pound of galantine of veal. You can get this *aux pistaches* at the Stores for 1s. 6d. a pound. Cut it into slices, but take care these do not break. Pass half a pound of tomatoes through a fine wire sieve. Place the tomato pulp in a small clean saucepan. Add to it a dessert-spoonful of vinegar, an onion stuck with a clove, half a gill of stock, and a little sifted sugar. Simmer slowly until it has reduced a little and thickened, then take out the onions, add pepper and salt to taste, and the sliced galantine. Make very hot and serve with a dish of dressed macaroni handed separately. If you can afford it a little sherry, say

77

half a wineglassful, is a great improvement to the above *entrèe*, but we never indulged in it.

We often had fowls and did them up in various ways. I always bought "soup fowls," because these, fresh and good, are nearly always obtainable from one and nine to two shillings each; whilst for an English fowl worthy the name you must pay at least two and nine or three shillings. *Poulet au riz* is a favourite dish of ours.

Here is the recipe :

Take a soup fowl and place it in a deep stewpan together with a large onion stuck with a clove, a bayleaf, twenty peppercorns, and a cupful of well-washed rice. Cover with water. Add salt to taste, put the lid on and bring very gently to the boil. Then draw the pan to the side of the fire, and let the contents simmer slowly for three hours. At the end of that time, take out the onions and peppercorns (these latter should be tied up in a muslin bag in all instances); and drain off and reserve the liquor. Dish up the fowl. Add to the rice from half an ounce to an ounce of butter, pepper and salt to taste, a grate of nutmeg, and the well-beaten yoke of an egg ; means permitting a pennyworth of cream is also an enormous improvement. Make very hot, garnish round the fowl, and serve as quickly as possible.

The liquor it was boiled in should be reserved in the larder till cold. Next day take off the cake of fat which will be found floating on the top, adding the latter to the fat bowl. Make the broth hot, garnish it with a little vermicelli or macaroni, and serve. If any of the rice remains from the previous night's dinner, it may be added to the soup and will form an excellent garnish. When tomatoes are to be had cheaply, say twopence or threepence a pound, treat an old fowl like this. *Poulet Portugaise :* Scale and rub a pound or a pound and a half of tomatoes through a fine wire sieve, add to the pulp a teaspoonful of sifted sugar, a tablespoonful of vinegar, pepper and salt to taste, and a little grated lemon peel, then reserve.

Place an ounce of either clarified beef dripping or butter in a clean deep stewpan. As soon as it melts add the fowl trussed as if for roasting, a large onion peeled and sliced, a bayleaf, and a pinch of sweet herbs. Fry for ten or twelve minutes, then remove the bayleaf, add the tomato pulp and a gill of stock, cover tightly, draw the pan to the side of the fire, and simmer very gently for two and a half or three hours. Take care the stock, etc., does not reduce, and keep basting the fowl, or else it will become dry and be spoilt. When quite done dish up on a hot dish. Boil up the gravy sharply and let it reduce a little in order to thicken. Then pour over and around the fowl and serve with fried potatoes and a dish of dressed macaroni handed separately.

Poulet à la Gitana is another good way of cooking a tough fowl.

Place a tablespoonful of oil in a clean saucepan. As soon as it gets hot, add the fowl trussed as if for boiling, a couple of thinly-sliced onions, as much garlic as will go on the point of a small knife, salt to taste, and a good dash of pepper ; fry all together, and then add a quarter of a pound of fat bacon, cut into neat squares. Draw the pan to the side of the fire and cook slowly for two hours or two hours and a half, basting the fowl every few minutes. When cooked, pour off the superfluous grease, if any, add a dessertspoonful of chutney to the onions, etc. Mix thoroughly. Dish up the fowl on a hot dish, garnish round with the onions, etc., and serve with plainly boiled rice handed instead of potatoes. To make a variety on the above dish, omit the chutney, add the pulp from three or four good-sized tomatoes in its place, make very hot and serve with the rice; rather more pepper and salt will be required in this latter case.

Ducks were things which we always found rather too expensive luxuries to indulge in. But ptarmigan, either roast or *en casserole*, black game, and wild fowl, such as teal, we often indulged in. When in season none of the above cost more than from ten-pence to one shilling each. Roasted plainly and served with a salad, they make a delightful change from ordinary fare.

I make it a rule to serve a second entrée of vege-tables every night, in the French fashion, and the reader will find this an economical plan to follow, as it helps to keep down the meat bill.

Here are a few recipes:

Chou à la Crême is one of the nicest. It is made like this:

Wash a cabbage well, then boil in salted water with a small onion stuck with a clove. When done, remove the clove from the onion, drain the cabbage till quite dry, and press both cabbage and onion through a hair sieve. Place half an ounce of butter in a clean stewpan, add the cabbage, a dust of white pepper and a pennyworth of cream, beat up lightly with a fork, make very hot; pile up in the centre of a hot dish. Garnish with fried croutons and serve.

Brussel tops *à la Française*, turnips *à la crème*, parsnips, *à la crème*, and brussels sprouts *à la crème* are all cooked in exactly the same way; and spinach, when cheap, is delicious treated in this fashion.

When carrots are cheap and you cannot get any other vegetable, try this:

Carottes à la Française. Scrape and trim a sufficient number of carrots all of a size. Place half an ounce of dripping in a clean stewpan, and when it melts add the carrots together with a slice of onion; fry for ten minutes, but take care that they do not burn. Then place on a fire-proof dish, just cover with well flavoured stock, and braise in the oven for two hours and a half, basting every now and then in order that they do not get dry. When done thicken the stock, if necessary, and serve.

Spanish onions braised in the same way are delightful. They will take rather longer to cook though, and of course the onion above mentioned must be omitted. Turnips and celery may be braised in the same way, but need not be previously fried. Artichokes, turnips, and parsnips are very nice served *au fromage*. Boil any of above vegetables, and when cooked, drain carefully, and pour over and around them half a pint of white sauce, to which has been added a couple of ounces of grated cheese. Garnish with croutons and serve. When cauliflowers are cheap, *Choufleur à la Polonaise* makes a nice vegetable *entrée*. Boil a cauliflower till cooked, and drain carefully. Place half an ounce of butter in a clean stewpan, when it melts add the cauliflower, and as much garlic as will go on the point of a small knife, turn gently in this for ten minutes, dust thickly with fried bread crumbs. Dish up on a hot dish and serve immediately.

When vegetables are very dear try *Riz à la Polonaise*. Place an ounce of either clarified beef dripping or butter in a clean stewpan ; when it oils add to it a minced onion or shalot, and fry for a couple of minutes; then add a teacupful of well-boiled and thoroughly dry rice. Fry till the rice is of a light fawny colour, but take care it does not burn. Add a little grated nutmeg and cheese, make very hot and serve hot.

For *Riz à la Florentine* omit the nutmeg and cheese, using in their place twopennyworth of picked shrimps. Make hot and serve.

For *Riz à la Turque*. Omit the shrimps. Add the cheese, a dozen split and stoned raisins, and a pinch of saffron. Make very hot and serve.

For *Riz à l'Indienne*. Omit the raisins and saffron. Add the cheese and a little cayenne pepper. Make hot and serve.

If you do not care for rice, Lentils, Butter beans and Peas are all cooked *à la Française*. Soak the lentils, butter beans, or green peas, as the case may be, for twenty-four hours. Then boil as usual in salted water. When cooked drain carefully. Place from half an ounce to an ounce of butter in a small stewpan. When it melts, add the beans, peas or lentils, with a little minced parsley, a dash of pepper, a pennyworth of cream, a few drops of lemon juice, and just a tiny pinch of sifted sugar, salt to taste. Toss lightly till very hot, and serve at once garnished with fried croutons. You can omit the cream if you like, but funds permitting it is a great improvement. If omitted add a little more lemon juice.

Fresh peas dressed like this are perfection, and the *Haricots Verts à la Française* are cooked in the same manner. When French beans are a penny a pound, or two pound for threehalfpence, you can see for yourself what a cheap *entrée* this is.

Cauliflower *au gratin*, macaroni *au gratin*, and macaroni cheese are all nice also, but as they are so well known ; I need not give the recipes. If you want a cold *entrée* try a *salade à la Française* of either lentils or butter beans. Boil the beans or lentils till tender. Drain thoroughly and leave till cold. Then add to them a grated shalot or small onion, a little finely-mixed parsley, a dash of pepper, salt if required, a tablespoonful of oil and half a tablespoonful of vinegar. Mix lightly and serve. Cold French beans, or cold peas, may be treated in the same way successfully. Add a pinch of sugar to the latter, or else use the remains of some mint sauce in place of the vinegar.

We used to turn all our scraps of vegetables to account in this way, so that nothing was wasted. Even cold potatoes did not escape. Try a potato salad made like this, and note that hard waxy potatoes make by far the best salad. Cut up a dozen cold boiled potatoes into slices about a quarter of an inch thick. Dust lightly with pepper and salt and place in a salad bowl. Add to them a finely-grated onion or shalot. Beat up the yolk of egg with a tablespoonful of oil and a pinch of salt till it thickens slightly, then add to it by degrees a tablespoonful of vinegar and a little minced parsley. Pour over the potatoes. Mix lightly but thoroughly and serve. If the potatoes are very flowery and won't slice properly, press them through a hair sieve, and when dressed, pile high in the centre of the salad bowl, and if possible garnish with a little sliced beetroot and quarters of hard-boiled egg. You can make another variety of this salad by adding to the potatoes a cold-boiled Spanish onion cut into slices.

When cucumbers are cheap, say from threehalfpence to twopence each, try cucumber *a la Poulette.* You are sure to like it. This is the recipe. Peel a cucumber thinly. Cut it into short lengths and scoop out the seeds. Then simmer slowly in half a pint of salted milk until quite tender. Drain carefully and reserve on a hot dish. Thicken the milk with half-an-ounce of flour and half-an-ounce of butter kneaded together, and when of the consistence of cream, add to it a little finely-minced parsley, the beaten yolk of an egg, a squeeze of lemon juice, and a tiny pinch of sifted sugar. Make very hot—but do not allow the sauce to actually boil after the egg has been added, or it will curdle —and serve at once.

If you would like cucumber *au Fromage,* omit the egg, lemon juice, and parsley, and add 2 ozs. of grated cheese. Make hot and serve. You can prepare cucumber *au jus* like this. Braise a peeled cucumber till tender in a little well-flavoured stock. Then dish it up on a hot dish. Thicken the stock in which it was cooked with a little flour and butter kneaded together, add a few drops of Parisian essence. Make very hot, pour over the cucumber and serve.

Vegetable marrows can be cooked in exactly the same way as any of the recipes given for cucumber, or can be stuffed with some parsley stuffing, and braised till tender in well-flavoured stock. When cooked thicken the stock with a bit of flour and butter, add a few drops of colouring essence. Make very hot, pour over the marrow and serve.

You must understand that we never indulged in any of these vegetable *entrées*, or for the matter of that in anything, except when the article in question was well in season and consequently cheap, and for this reason I always kept a bag of lentils, a bag of dried green peas, and a bag of butter beans in the house, because they form an excellent standby, and can be used, not only to form vegetable *entrées*, but for purées, etc.

For instance we often had mutton cutlets, and a purée of green peas in the depth of winter. Soak the dried green peas for a day and a half. Then boil them with an onion and a little dried mint, when thoroughly tender drain and press through a fine sieve. Return the purée thus obtained to a clean saucepan, add to it a bit of butter the size of a walnut, a tablespoonful of milk, a dust of pepper, and a pinch of sifted sugar. Make very hot, arrange round the cutlets as you would a wall of

85

mashed potato, and serve. If you can afford it a
1d. worth of cream is an enormous improvement to
this purée. You can make a purée of the butter
beans in precisely the same manner, but these
require less soaking, say for two or three hours.
If liked a squeeze of lemon juice may be added to
the purée together with the sifted sugar.

Veal cutlets with a purée of lentils is another nice
dish. Prepare the purée as directed above. Use
the *green* lentils for this, but bear in mind that you
must soak them for at least a day and a half.

A purée of parsnips is very nice with a piece of
braised beef. Boil the parsnips till tender in salted
water, then pass them through a fine wire sieve.
Place the purée thus obtained in a clean saucepan
with a bit of butter the size of a walnut, a dab of
white pepper, a pinch of sifted sugar, a dessertspoonful of milk, and a few drops of lemon juice.
Make very hot and serve.

Turnips may be treated in the same way, and
so may white artichokes.

When green artichokes are in season, they make
a delicious vegetable course. Boil plainly in salted
water, and serve with a little oiled butter handed
separately.

Braised salsify is delicious also, and a bundle will
serve you twice, as I find that servants do not
care for the pronounced flavour of this vegetable.
It should be braised as directed for carrots, but
omit the frying process.

The vegetables we were obliged to avoid were,
in winter, seakale, and in summer, asparagus,
because fond as we were of them, they are but

rarely low enough in price to permit of our indulging in them, more than perhaps once in a season. This, of course, applies more to asparagus than seakale.

With fruit I had to be even more particular, since I made it a rule, from which I never swerve, no matter how much I may be tempted, never to indulge in any which is not thoroughly sound.

It is a very poor policy which saves its house-keeping money at the expense of large doctor's bills.

Other things I have served whenever practicable are *savouries*.

Now these make a nice finish to a dinner, and most men are fond of them to a degree. More-over, they need not add one iota to the expenses if you go the right way to work about it.

For instance, when the bones for the weekly stock arrive from the butcher's, look them over carefully, and extract every particle of marrow from those possessing any. Use this for marrow toast, either plain or with a good dash of cayenne to add to its piquancy.

When the fish makes its appearance, if herrings or mackerel, extract the soft roes. Place a bit of butter in a clean frying-pan; add the roes together with a dash of pepper and salt, to taste, and when cooked, arrange neatly on squares of hot toast and send to table. A few drops of lemon juice are a great improvement to soft roes on toast.

Croustades, or *croutes de laitances*, are, as a rule, greatly beloved by the sterner sex. Here is the recipe:

Cook the roes as described above, then place in

a mortar, with a tiny bit of butter, a dash of cayenne pepper, a little salt if needed, and a few drops of lemon juice, pound to a paste, spread on hot fried rounds of bread. Dust with pepper again. Place in a hot oven for five minutes and serve.

Marrow first cooked and then treated in the same way is also excellent.

Chicken liver makes another delightful savoury. Cook the liver with a bit of butter and a dash of pepper. Then pound in the mortar with a bit of butter, a little cayenne, a few drops of lemon juice, and a grate of nutmeg. When of a pastelike consistency spread either on toast or on fried rounds of bread. Place in a hot oven for ten minutes, and then serve.

Anchovy crusts are made by spreading a little anchovy paste on a couple of rounds of fried bread, dust with pepper and serve.

When you have a couple of sardines left over from a tin, don't throw them away, cut two strips of stale bread, and either toast and spread them with butter or else fry till of a light golden brown hue; drain, place a sardine upon each, dust with pepper, place in the oven for five or six minutes and serve.

Any tiny scrap of fish left from dinner or breakfast may also be turned into a savoury, if pounded in the mortar as described above, seasoned highly and spread upon rounds of fried bread or toast.

Failing any of these, there is no nicer savoury than shrimps on toast or *croutes aux crevettes*. Buy a pennyworth of picked shrimps, have ready a couple of squares of toast, or else two or three tiny rounds of fried bread. Make the shrimps hot in a tiny bit of butter, then arrange neatly on the croutes or toast, dust with cayenne pepper, and serve. When you have had game of some sort any tiny scraps which may be remaining, even if they amount but to a solitary ounce, can be turned into a couple of dainty savouries if treated in the same way, and pounded in a mortar with a bit of butter about the size of a small walnut, a dash of pepper and salt, and a couple of drops of lemon juice. Spread upon tiny squares of toast or else upon a couple of tiny circular croutons. Dust with cayenne pepper, place in a hot oven for a few minutes, and send to table.

Failing fish, game, or any other scraps, utilize an egg as follows :—

Boil an egg till perfectly hard, throw it into cold water, and then remove the shell and cut into halves. Take out the yolk, place it in a mortar with a dust of salt and pepper, a drop or two of lemon juice and a few drops of essence of anchovy, or else a tiny teaspoonful of anchovy paste; work to a paste, use to fill the halved egg. Dust with cayenne pepper, garnish each half with a tiny sprig of parsley, and send to table.

With the cayenne pepper omitted, this makes a good *hors d'œuvre.*

Another way to utilize an egg is to make the above paste, spread it upon two squares of toast or else upon a couple of fried croutes, mince the white finely, scatter on top and serve.

If liked, this savoury may be made hot in the oven for a few minutes before being sent to table.

Tomato savouries are very nice. Take a tiny tomato,

scald, cut it in half and scoop out the pulp, fill the centre with the egg mixture above referred to, garnish each half with a tiny sprig of parsley and serve, or mix the pulp with the egg mixture, add a little more lemon juice and plenty of salt, and serve.

With the pepper omitted, these, too, make a nice *hors d'œuvre*, but *hors d'œuvres* were not things we ever indulged in except when we had a dinner party.

Sardines make a good savoury or *hors d'œuvre* if dusted thickly with pepper, and placed on a square of toast spread with marrow made hot in the oven and served at once. But enough of savouries. What gave me most trouble at first was the

PUDDINGS.

Milk puddings, so beloved of the average Englishwoman who possesses small means, did not appeal to me at all, because it is a patent fact that you cannot make a milk pudding without milk, and milk costs 4d. a quart. True, skim milk is obtainable at 2d. a quart, but then the puddings are never so satisfactory.

I found that steamed puddings of various kinds suited my purse and purpose better, and moreover, always looked dainty ; a virtue which cannot be claimed for the average pudding baked in a pie dish.

A cream of rice, commonly called *Riz à la Francaise* is particularly nice. Here is the recipe. Wash four ounces of rice, and then place it in a saucepan with a pint of sweetened water, a little grated nutmeg and a bit of cinnamon, or a pinch of powdered cinnamon. When quite tender, by which time the rice should have absorbed all the water, add to it a little grated lemon peel, or a few bits of chopped candied peel, a tiny pinch of salt, a gill of milk, and when cool, two well-beaten eggs, yolks and whites together. Stir well ; fill a well-greased mould with the mixture, tie down, steam for an hour. Turn out carefully and serve with a little jam sauce poured round it. Make the sauce thus :—

To every two tablespoonfuls of jam add one of water, make very hot. Press through a heated gravy strainer over the pudding and serve. Tapioca, semolina, and sago can all be treated after the above recipe, and make delicious puddings.

You can vary the flavour by using a few drops of almond, or vanilla, or lemon essence instead of the nutmeg and cinnamon which are more suitable to the rice.

You can make a delightful bread-pudding like this. It is known as *Poudin Viennoise.* Take some slices of stale bread, place them in a basin, and pour over them half-a-pint, or more, according to the amount of bread, of perfectly boiling milk. Skim milk answers admirably for this.

Cover, and let the bread soak for half an hour. Then add a tiny pinch of salt and beat up vigorously with a fork until all the milk is absorbed. Add sugar to suit your own taste, and enough white sauce to form a light batter. Leave till cold ; then add a little powdered cinnamon or a few drops of vanilla essence, whichever you like best, the well-beaten yolks of two eggs, and finally the whites whisked to a stiff froth. Mix thoroughly; use to fill a well-greased mould. Steam for an hour and a half, and serve with jam sauce poured over and around. *Note.*—This pudding may be improved by the addition of a couple of ounces of well-chopped raisins and currants, or an ounce of chopped candied peel, or glacé cherries.

Golden syrup may be used instead of sugar when sweetening.

Brown bread pudding is very nice. Make it thus:—Take six ounces of stale brown bread crumbs, pour over them half a pint of boiling (skim) milk, add sugar to taste, and then beat in by degrees the yolks of two eggs, and the whites of three whisked separately. Add the juice of half a lemon and half an ounce of finely chopped candied peel. Fill a greased mould with the mixture. Steam for two hours, and serve with a sweet white sauce flavoured with either lemon juice or vanilla.

Vanilla soufflé is a very dainty and at the same time cheap sweet. It is made thus:

Take two tablespoonfuls of flour and mix with them two tablespoonfuls of cornflour. Moisten with a little cold milk and water. Place half a pint of milk in a clean enamelled saucepan. As soon as it boils add the cornflour, etc., and stir briskly until quite thick, then add sugar to taste, and remove the pan from the fire as soon as the sugar has melted. Next add the well-beaten yolks of two eggs, a few drops of either vanilla or lemon essence, and finally the whites of three eggs whisked to a stiff froth; stir these in as lightly as possible. Fill a mould with the mixture, and bake for twenty-five minutes in a very hot oven. Serve with jam sauce, handed separately.

When apples are cheap, *Apple souffle* is to be recommended.

Boil an ounce of well-washed rice in some skim milk flavoured with cinnamon until every drop of the milk is well absorbed. By this time the rice should be thoroughly well cooked. Press it through a fine wire sieve into a clean basin. Peel, core, and slice six apples, parboil them, and then add to the rice, and beat to a fine pulp. Add an ounce of sugar and a few drops of either vanilla or lemon essence. Then stir in by degrees the well-beaten yolks of two eggs, mix and finally add the whites of three eggs whipped to a stiff froth. This must be done as lightly as possible. Use the mixture to fill a well-greased mould. Turn out carefully and serve with vanilla sauce. All white sauces for puddings can be made thus : Work an ounce of butter with an ounce of flour, and then mix to a paste with a little cold milk or water, place in a clean saucepan, and add to it gradually half a pint of warm milk—skim or fresh, it does not matter which—stir briskly till quite smooth and creamy.

For a white sauce add sifted sugar to taste, and a few drops of any flavouring essence best liked.

For a brown or brandy sauce, use coarse brown sugar, and add a little rum or brandy, whichever is preferred. Make very hot and serve.

Either of these sauces is enormously improved by the addition of the well-beaten yolk of an egg, but the sauce must not be allowed to actually boil again after the egg is added, or it will curdle and be quite spoilt.

Sherry or port wine sauce is made by adding

half a glassful of port or sherry to the above sauce. When made with the brown sugar, a little grated nutmeg or cinnamon will be found an improvement.

Beignets à la Portugaise are a very nice sweet for a small dinner party.

Put three ounces of well-washed rice into a clean saucepan. Add to it a tiny pinch of salt, half a pint of fresh or skimmed milk, two ounces of sugar, half an ounce of butter, a little powdered cinnamon, and the grated rind of half a lemon; simmer gently over a slow fire for three-quarters of an hour, by which time the rice should have absorbed all moisture. Leave till quite cool, and then add the well-beaten yolks of two eggs, and finally the whites, whisked separately.

Leave again till quite cold, then make into balls about the size of a very small tangerine. Place a tiny spoonful of marmalade or jam in the centre of each, roll in sweetened egg and bread crumbs, and fry in deep fat till of a light golden colour. Take out quickly, drain carefully, powder with sifted sugar, and serve at once. *Note.*—Don't fry too many at one time.

Russian Pudding.—Take four ounces of bread crumbs, four ounces of flour, two ounces of suet, and two ounces of coarse brown sugar; mix well together, then add the grated rind of a lemon, half an ounce of finely-chopped candied peel, and enough golden syrup to mix to a stiff paste; add a little milk also, if liked; finally, add the yolks of two eggs and the whites of three mixed to a stiff froth; fill a greased mould with the mixture, steam for two hours and a half, and serve with sweet brown sauce.

American plum tart is, as children would say, "awfully good." Here is the recipe :

Line any fancy, fireproof china dish with some thin crisp slices of buttered toast. Fill up the centre with stoned cooked plums, and scatter thickly with Demarara sugar, repeat the toast, plums and sugar till the dish is quite full. Scatter plenty of sugar on top and bake in a moderate oven for thirty minutes. Serve either hot or cold. A little whipped and sweetened cream on top is a vast improvement to this pudding.

When funds were low, as often as not, we indulged in jelly for a sweet. A pint packet costs but threepence halfpenny, and one can scarcely make a pudding worthy the name for so low as sum as that.

Sometimes when apples or oranges were cheap we indulged in apple or orange fritters. *Note.*—Make your batter at least an hour before you want to use it, and use tepid water, *not* milk, when mixing. This rule also holds good when making batter for pancakes.

We did not indulge in pastry, except on the rarest of occasions, for to make really first-class puff pastry, you must have a plenitude of fresh butter, and as fresh butter is expensive, we did without pastry, and were none the worse for our abstention.

One of our favourite sweets was apples cooked after this fashion.

Wash and dry half a dozen apples. Do not peel them. Remove the core by means of a vegetable cutter (if you don't possess an apple corer). Fill the centre of each with a little strawberry or other jam, and bake in the usual way. Dust with sifted sugar and serve.

Tapioca cream is another nice sweet. Try it. It is made thus :

Boil four ounces of tapioca till quite tender in some sweetened water with a little grated nutmeg. Then drain carefully. Spread the bottom of a fancy dish with a layer of jam. As soon as the tapioca is cold, add to the jam, pour over the whole the contents of a fivepenny jar of cream and serve. You can improve the appearance of this dish by, if liked, garnishing it with half an ounce of blanched almonds cut into strips, and stuck in lengthwise. The remains of a cold tapioca pudding are excellent, utilized as above, and sago also can be treated with advantage in the same manner.

Any stale cake which you may have on hand will make a delightful pudding, if soaked in a little skim milk, and then beaten up lightly with a fork; add the yolks of two eggs, and lastly the whites whisked to a stiff froth separately. Fill a greased mould with the mixture, and steam for an hour. Serve with sweet white or brown sauce, according to whether the pudding in question is of sponge, or currant cake.

Stale ginger-bread makes a first-class pudding. Soak it first in half a pint of skimmed milk. Then beat up well with a fork. Add to it a couple of dessertspoonfuls of golden syrup, the yolks of two eggs, and the whites from the same whisked separately to a stiff froth. Use to fill a well-greased mould, steam for an hour and a half, and serve with a cinnamon sauce, made by adding a little powdered cinnamon to some sweet brown sauce. If cinnamon is not liked use nutmeg, or a spoonful of brandy.

Biscuit pudding may be made in precisely the same way, but the biscuits will require rather longer soaking. Ordinary broken sweet biscuits can be bought at any grocers or at the Stores for three-pence a pound, and macaroons and ratafias if broken are to be had as low as sixpence a pound.

When funds are very low, quite an acceptable sweet can be made thus: Stamp out some rounds from a couple of slices of stale bread, soak for a few minutes in sweetened milk, flavoured with vanilla. Dust with sugar and fry in deep fat. Take out quickly. Drain carefully, spread with jam, place a little cream or a few chopped almonds on top of each, and serve.

Rounds of stale cake treated in this way are even nicer. Especially sponge cake, but if the latter is very stale, it should be first soaked for some time in a little milk, or even sweetened water, before being fried.

Nice little *Chocolate Tartlets* can be made thus: Buy half a dozen penny patty cases. You can get these at almost any confectioner's. Melt two-pennyworth of chocolate in a saucepan, together with a gill of milk and a little dessertspoonful of cornflour; when quite smooth and of the consistency of very thick cream, use to fill the tartlets. Leave till cold and serve with a tiny bit of whipped cream on the top of each. Omit the latter if considered too expensive.

The foregoing are a sample of the dishes we

97

indulged in for dinner; and now and again when funds were getting low, or we had been entertaining and I had consequently been obliged to spend rather more than usual, I used to try and think out new dishes for myself, and I am bound to say invariably succeeded.

For instance, when we had a little, just a very little, cold chicken left, I used to treat it like this:

Cut the remains of a cold chicken into neat tiny squares, and free them from skin. Have ready four ounces of cooked macaroni, cut into short lengths; mix with the pieces of chicken. Have ready half a pint of bechamel sauce, and when it is very hot stir into it the well-beaten yolk of an egg, then add the chicken, macaroni, etc. Make hot again but do not allow the mixture to actually boil, or the egg will curdle. Serve with fried potatoes. The above will be found an excellent way of utilizing any scraps of cold chicken which may be too small in quantity to produce a dish unaided.

One of my principal difficulties was the

BREAKFASTS,

because, you see, with my limited housekeeping money, to indulge in eggs and bacon, unless we were content to have the latter of inferior quality, was out of the question. I only allowed the servants a plain (*i.e.*, bread and butter) breakfast except on Sundays, when they had an egg or a bloater or a kipper for a relish. But for my husband something more substantial was an absolute necessity, since his lunch was a lunch in name only.

Remembering that variety is the spice of life, I determined to let this meal vary as much as possible. So one morning I gave kidneys (two New Zealand kidneys, cost 2½d. the pair). Split, fry, and fill the centre with a scrap of *maître d'hotel* butter, or anchovy butter. The recipe for the first-named you will find earlier in the book ; for the second, work a teaspoonful of anchovy paste with a rather larger teaspoonful of butter. *Note.*—What is left over will make a savoury for the evening's dinner if spread upon fried *croutès*, or on two tiny squares of toast.

Another morning dried haddock with egg sauce formed the *pièce de résistance*. Wipe the haddock well with a damp cloth ; place in a saucepan with half a pint of skim milk ; cook slowly. When done take out and dish up on a hot dish, and reserve in the oven. Thicken the milk with a little flour and a bit of butter kneaded together, stir till of the consistency of cream, then add a teaspoonsful of French mustard and a hard-boiled egg chopped into tiny squares. Make hot, and serve separately in a sauce boat. Most cooks pour this sauce over the haddock, but if the latter is kept dry, any scraps left may be turned into a savoury for the evening's dinner if pounded in a mortar with a bit of butter, a dash of Cayenne pepper, a squeeze of lemon juice, and a little grated nutmeg. Spread on fried *croutés* or squares of toast, make hot in the oven and serve.

Another morning we had scrambled eggs, or eggs and bacon. Another kippers or the plebeian bloater, of which we are both very fond. When any fish was

99

left from the previous night's dinner we turned it into fish cakes or into kedjeree ; and on Sundays we generally indulged in a small tin of smoked sardines, price 4½d. Every morning we had porridge, sometimes made from oatmeal, sometimes from Quaker oats. The latter are simply delicious when properly made, if served with a little coarse sugar and butter, or with a little golden syrup.

Occasionally, when we had a loin of mutton (New Zealand, of course) for dinner, I cut off a couple of chops and placed them in a marinade until the morning but one after. They were then grilled, and were a most welcome addition to the breakfast table.

Marmalade I always had on hand, or else jam or golden syrup, for most men like something sweet as a finish to breakfast.

Then, too, I always insisted upon a rack full of crisp, golden brown toast, and what was left of this reappeared at dinner. A dish of stewed beef kidney —half a pound of the latter only costs 4d., and is ample for two people—was a favourite dish of ours ; and when apples are cheap, a dish of roasted apples is by no means to be despised for breakfast.

In short, I varied our matutinal fare as much as I possibly could, and in the long run you will find that this plan is by far the most economical one to pursue, as it spells " less waste." Serving the same thing up week in week out means that the best part of it gets left, whereas if something different makes its appearance each morning it is pretty nearly sure to be appreciated and to disappear. Here are a few of our breakfast *menus* :—

Porridge and golden syrup.
Stewed beef kidneys.
Potato cakes.
Toast.   Marmalade.
Coffee.

———

Porridge (made from butter beans).
Scrambled eggs.
Hot rolls (home-made).
Toast.   Jam.
Cocoa.

———

Porridge (Quaker oats).
Haddock.   Egg sauce.
Fried toast.
Golden syrup.
Tea.

———

Porridge (made from coarse oatmeal).
Kidneys with anchovy butter.
Fried potatoes.
Toast.   Marmalade.
Coffee.

———

Porridge with sugar and butter.
Bacon and eggs.
Potato cakes.
Toast.   Jam.
Tea.

———

Porridge (Quaker oats).
Grilled bloaters.
Buttered toast.
Marmalade.
Cocoa.

———

Porridge.
Kedjeree.
Hot buttered cakes.
Toast.   Jam.
Coffee.

These of course are but samples taken at random. In the winter we often indulged in the fried toast above referred to. This is made exactly like the square croutons used for garnishing, but is awarded less frying, as it should go to table crisp, yet soft inside. The hot cakes mentioned above sound extravagant, but are not so in reality. Add a good pinch of salt to half a pound of self-raising flour, rub in two ounces of clarified beef dripping, mix to the right consistency by means of a little water, milk and water, or milk, shape into rounds, bake in a fairly hot oven for half an hour, split, butter, and serve. With the addition of two ozs. sugar and an extra two ozs. of dripping, these will do excellently for afternoon tea ; raisons, currants, or a little spice may be added at discretion. Of course the above is only a recipe for very plain and inexpensive cakes indeed. If you require something more elaborate you can easily achieve it by substituting butter for the clarified dripping, and mixing with milk instead of water. The potato cakes are made like this : Take a sufficient number of cold boiled potatoes and mash them well with a bit of butter about the size of a large walnut, a little minced parsley, pepper and salt to taste, a little milk, and if liked, the well-beaten yolk of an egg. Form into small rounds and bake in a moderate oven till of a light golden brown, serve as hot as possible. If egged and bread crumbed, these may be fried in deep fat, and you will then have potato rissoles. Drain carefully on a clean kitchen paper before serving.

When baked in the oven these cakes may be

split and buttered if liked. Egg pie is a delicious breakfast dish. It is made like this. Boil four eggs till perfectly hard. Throw into cold water and take off the shells. Then cut into slices and reserve on a plate. Mash some cold potatoes as directed above for potato cake. Spread a layer of this in the bottom of a small pie-dish. Have ready a sliced fried onion, drained free from the fat it was cooked in. Spread a little of this on the potato. Add some of the sliced egg and a little white sauce, then more potato, and repeat these layers till the dish is quite full, finish with a layer of potato. Scatter bread crumbs thickly on top, put a few bits of butter here and there, and place in the oven till very hot, by which time the top of the pie should be well browned, then serve.

And here is another nice way of treating hard boiled eggs, it is known as *œufs à la Royale*.

Boil two or three eggs till perfectly hard. Throw into cold water and take off the shells. Have ready some bread crumbs, well seasoned with salt and pepper, grate a little shalot into this and mix with it a little minced parsley. Dip each egg first into some beaten egg and next into the mixture. Fry in deep fat, take out quickly, drain carefully, and serve as hot as possible. Cold potatoes fried in bacon fat are very nice with eggs cooked after the foregoing manner.

Apropos of bacon let me advise you never to try that of a cheaper quality, the best and best only, is the only sort you should indulge in. Of course the very best can also be had very cheaply, by taking a large quantity at a time. But this is a plan which does not commend itself except to those having a large household to cater for, as otherwise it is apt to become rancid long before it can be used up ; or else to avoid this you have to eat bacon *ad nauseam* till you loathe the very name. My own plan is to purchase half a pound of the best back or streaky bacon, which costs from 10d. to 1s. per pound, and this suffices to give bacon twice a week for breakfast (we only eat a very little), or once for breakfast and once for use in some dinner dish. Have it cut into the thinnest possible rashers, and see that this is done at the time you buy it.

But enough of breakfasts. This is how we managed about

LUNCHEONS.

My husband being out all day we only had a meat luncheon as a rule on Saturdays, when he came home for that meal. On other days in the week we had a thick substantial soup followed by a substantial pudding. I have already told you how we managed about the stock, and the amount we made served us all the week round for luncheon and dinner.

I varied the soup each day as much as possible and the pudding also, but I always took care that both were *substantial*. Clear soup followed by a baked custard won't enable anybody to go from breakfast till dinner (tea I don't count) without feeling hungry.

Sometimes we had suet dumplings cooked in the plain stock, followed by rice pudding. Sometimes a rice soup, followed by a roly poly jam or treacle pudding. Occasionally I bought a small hock of bacon, and then the liquor it was cooked in we used for pea soup, and followed the latter up with a bread pudding. In winter time we often had potato soup, succeeded by the Russian pudding, the recipe for which I have already given you. Then we had *Potage bonne femme*, or *Croute au pot*, followed by apple pudding or baked treacle tart. Lentil soup or currant dumplings, or green pea soup and a boiled batter pudding, eaten with coarse sugar, we often indulged in. Of course we occasionally had meat for lunch also, but the above are fair specimens of what our lunches generally were, and I am bound to say I have never yet had a servant who grumbled at theirs. The

SERVANTS' MEALS

I arranged like this. In the mornings they had tea or cocoa for breakfast, with as much bread and butter as they chose to eat, and an egg or fish on Sundays. Their luncheon was the same as mine. For tea they could have a dripping cake hot or cold, if they chose to make it, or else a little golden syrup or jam with their bread and butter. Occasionally, too, when bloaters were cheap, they had one apiece for tea. Their dinner was the same as our own with the sole exceptions of fruit and savouries. We never have more than two or three of the latter made unless we are expecting guests, as to relegate them to the kitchen means, in other words, throwing them away, and fruit of course I could not afford to buy for the servants, although now and again, when apples or oranges were cheap, I gave them one each on Sundays.

By feeding them exactly on the same lines as ourselves I prevented two of the chief drawbacks to economical housekeeping, viz. : waste and grumbling. Nothing was wasted because every scrap was always eaten up, and certainly no servant can reasonably grumble if she is given the same fare as her master and mistress.

CHAPTER XI

OF course with limited means at my command anything in the nature of a store cupboard worthy of the name was quite out of the question. Nevertheless, though *caviar, pâté de foie gras, fonds d'artichants, glâcé cherries,* and all other delicacies, which are such a help towards providing dainties in an emergency were beyond my reach, I determined to have the best substitute I could command. I invested therefore in the following articles, and called the receptacle they were kept in a store cupboard, and every Saturday before I went shopping I examined its contents carefully, and replaced those of my "stores" which showed signs of running out. Moreover, whenever I found myself possessed of a spare shilling I always expended it in the replenishment of my cupboard, and by degrees got together quite a host of dainties which were simply invaluable when we had people to dine with us or when I wished to augment the dinner.

The following is a list of the things wherewith I started the foundation of my cupboard. I give the store prices of each article in case you may wish to emulate me :—

2 lbs. of rice, 1½d. a lb., 3d. The 1½d. rice is quite as good as that which is dearer, but it is smaller grained and requires a great deal of

washing. 2 lbs. of tapioca, 2d. a lb., 4d. 2 lbs. of
sago, 4d. 2 lbs. of dried green peas, 4d. 2 lbs. of
red lentils, 4d. A 7 lb. bag of American butter
beans, 1s. A bottle of soy for colouring, 5½d. A
bottle of vanilla essence, 6d. 4 packets of jelly
crystals, assorted flavours, 3½d. a packet, 1s. 2d. A
bottle of essence of rennet for making junkets, 6d.
A bottle of chutney, 6d. A jar of French mustard,
4½d. A jar of anchovy paste, 6d. A jar of bloater
paste for savouries, only for use when we had
absolutely nothing else, 6d. 2 lbs. of raisins, 6d.
2 lbs. of currants, 6d. 6d. worth of mixed candied
peel. A big tin of golden syrup, 10d. A 7 lb. jar
of cooking jam, 1s. 2d., 3d. is charged for jar and
allowed when it is returned. A 7 lb. jar of
marmalade, 1s. 2d., jar charged for same rate as
jam. A small bottle essence almond, 3½d. A
bottle of vinegar, 7d. A large bottle of oil, 10d. A
small bottle Tarragon vinegar, 4d. A small bottle
Chili vinegar, 4½d. These latter are only to be
used when making sauces ; and, as only a teaspoonful or at the outside two, is required, they last
an indefinite time. They must always be carefully
corked after using, or the contents will be spoilt.
A bottle of Harvey sauce, price 5d. A bottle of
mushroom catsup, 5d. A bottle of pickled walnuts,
to be used in making entrées, 6d. A bottle of
olives, 5d., also to be used for entrées. A 1s. box of
brown dessicated soup. This is simply invaluable
for thickening gravies, or producing soup (when
stock is unobtainable) at a few minutes' notice. A
1d. packet each of dried mint, sage, and mixed
sweet herbs. A 1d. worth of bay leaves. 2 ounces

of cloves, 1½d. 2 ounces powdered cinnamon, 2d. 2d. worth of mace. 3d. worth of nutmeg. A 3½d. tin of allspice. 6d. worth of broken sweet biscuits. These latter for puddings, but only to be used when we had a dinner-party. A 6d. jar of preserved ginger. A large pot of red currant jelly, 7d. 2 lbs. of barley, 4d.; and, these two latter we kept separately. 2 ounces of garlic, 1½d. 2 ounces of shalots, 1½d., and a 6d. packet of isinglass.

The total of these things only came to just £1 1s., and with their aid I found that all the simpler kinds of French cookery and dainty entrées were well within my reach; but I was careful, as you must be, if you wish to keep house successfully, never to let any one thing run completely out. When lemons are dear, a bottle of essence of lemon, which must however be used with the greatest discrimination, may be added to the store cupboard.

But to go on. Perhaps one of the greatest difficulties I had to contend with was the oilman's bill.

You must remember that to keep a house really sweet and clean, one requires a plenitude of such things as soap, soda, beeswax, and turpentine, hearthstone, blacklead, etc., etc., and, although these things are in themselves cheap, they yet mount up in the course of a year to a very pretty total.

It is by far the cheapest to buy soda in the 6d. bags, these contain 28 lbs. But if you wish to be successfully economical you must not let your maid have the whole bag at once to do as she likes with.

If you do the best part of that soda will find its way down the kitchen sink, for she will take a handful when a bit the size of a walnut is all that is required. It is no use *asking* her to be careful. I have found that out by long experience, and now I always tell my maids how bad soda is for the hands, and how it coarsens and reddens them. If you try this plan you will find that soda lasts out marvellously; what they won't do for you they will for their own vanity's sake.

Sometimes even this has no effect, in which case your best plan will be to keep the large bag of soda under lock and key, giving out just enough to last a week.

Don't buy furniture polish or cream.

For ordinary and oak furniture turpentine and beeswax is by far the cheapest polishing medium you can employ, and articles of furniture which have been French polished, such as drawing-room furniture, pianos, etc., if well rubbed up with an old silk handkerchief, should not require any other polish.

For polishing brass there is nothing better than a little of one of the numerous brass polishes sold now. Mind, I said "a *little*," for if a quantity of this polish, which contains vitriol, is used and imperfectly rubbed off, it will only produce verdigris, and in the end the article in question will look worse instead of better.

For cleaning silver or electro plate nothing can excel ordinary whitening mixed to a paste by means

of a little water, methylated spirits, or gin, either of
the latter for preference—though they add a trifle
to the expense—because they produce such a fine
polish, and moreover in the case of plated articles
do not rub off the plating, as many powders are apt
to do. Looking-glasses requiring a special cleaning
should be damped with a little methylated spirit
and then well polished with an old silk handkerchief. A little vinegar, only a few drops are
required, added to the cold water in which the
table glass is rinsed, will brighten and make it
easier to polish. For cleaning knives I have found
finely powdered bath brick answer quite as well as
knife polish. It may perhaps be urged that the
former tends to scratch the steel, but if rubbed only
backwards and forwards instead of up and down
and all ways, this is not the case, and a bath brick
of large size only costs a $\frac{1}{2}$d., whereas knife polish
is 5d. per tin.

Take the brick, scrape a little on to the knife
board and polish in the ordinary way. For the
front door steps, whitening is to be preferred to
hearth stones as it gives a much better colour and
dries more quickly, but for the area steps, the
hearthstone is better as it does not rub off so
quickly, nor need renewing so often.

Always have a leather to give the final polish to
the windows when cleaning the latter. A cloth is
apt to leave unsightly bits of fluff behind it and
make the windows look as though the cleaning had
been very imperfectly done indeed. Boot cream is
often rather a large item if the master of the house
wears patent boots. Try beeswax and turpentine

next time, it will be found to answer equally well, and only requires plenty of elbow grease to put as fine a polish as the heart of man could desire on to even the dullest pair of patent leather boots.

If carpets have got dull and faded looking, try rubbing them up with a cloth wrung out of tepid water to which had been added a little ammonia, this will fetch up the colour.

White enamelled furniture which has got dirty and yellow looking may be improved by being washed with powdered whitening; use the latter as if it were soap, and then wash off well. Don't indulge in a regular spring cleaning unless you can afford the services of a charwoman in addition to your regular servants. If you do you will only get into a muddle and make your husband thoroughly uncomfortable. Keep the house absolutely clean all the year round, and when the time for leaving off fires occurs, let the sweep do one chimney per day, on the day in which that special room has its usual weekly turning out; by this plan you will get all the rooms cleaned in turn without putting extra work on to the servants, or in any way disorganizing your household.

Have the carpets, etc., beaten while you are away for your annual holiday. One of the tradesmen's men are generally glad to do this for an odd shilling or two.

All this time we have been getting further and further away from our original subject, the oilman's bill. However, to go back once more.

If you use oil at all, let me advise you to purchase the best, and the best only both for upstairs use and down. It is a very poor kind of economy which may result in burning down the house. When buying soap, get half a dozen bars at a time, put it in a cool, dry place and let it dry slowly, soap thus hardened lasts quite twice as long as if used when new. If you require a disinfectant at any time, there is nothing better or cheaper than a 1d. worth of chloride of lime, and though this perhaps smells unpleasantly, yet the odour soon goes off and it does its work thoroughly and well.

Failing this, or if you really dislike it, get 2d. worth of permanganate of potash crystals, and dissolve a few of these in a pail of boiling water, use as required. *Note.*—Lock up the remainder of the crystals when done with, for future use. Don't leave them about for the servants to waste or misuse. Buy the cheapest blacklead you can get. The so called " stove polishes " with high sounding names have all blacklead as their basis, and you only pay extra for the name, *not* the article.

You will find it cheaper in the long run to buy your turpentine and beeswax ready mixed, as less is required when it is of the right creamy consistency. Untrained servants are apt to overdo the beeswax when left to themselves, but this is impossible if you purchase it ready for use. The cost is fivepence a small, tenpence a large, tin at almost any oilman's, or at the stores or grocers.

Twopennyworth of rock ammonia should always find a place on the kitchen shelves, as it is invaluable for so many things, taking stains out of dresses, coats, etc., and carpets or upholstered furniture.

A bit added to the water in which the silver is

washed will greatly enhance the brightness of the latter. To

WASH AT HOME

with anything like comfort is not the easiest thing in the world.

Nevertheless it can be done if method obtains. This is how we managed:

The clothes, so far as possible, were all sorted on Saturday evenings, with the exception of the sheets.

On Sunday nights we slightly soaped and put them in to soak in soapy water, and then on Monday mornings the fine white things, such as sheets, towels, pillow slips, and handkerchiefs were all washed first, and then the flannels of all sorts quickly, the dusters and kitchen rubbers being done afterwards in the lather from the sheets, etc., as this tends to save the soap; the tea cloths, meat cloths, fish cloths, and glass cloths being, of course, done separately in fresh water.

The copper fire was always lighted the very first thing in the morning, and by ten o'clock the first lot of things were always on to boil. Here are some hints if you would wash at home successfully. Don't use dark blue, the pale is much to be preferred. We did not do any starched things at home, but if you wish to, add a pinch of powdered borax in your starch, and you will find it an improvement. To take ink, tea, or wine stains out of table linen, etc., nothing can excel salts of lemon. A little paraffin added to the water in which the dusters are put to soak, and afterwards to that in which they are washed, will help to get the dirt out more quickly.

Never attempt to boil coloured and white things together, or the results may be disastrous.

Never allow your maid on any pretext, save that of illness, to leave any of the washing over " for next day," I mean things which are already in the water and partly washed. If you do your linen will soon be spoilt.

If you possess a lawn, no matter how small it may be, always utilize it to bleach the linen, nothing, no, not all the chemicals in the world will make it such a good colour, or give such satisfactory results. It must be sprinkled occasionally from time to time as it gets over dry.

Linen which has got over dry must also be sprinkled before being ironed or mangled.

When about to iron test the iron with a bit of paper, this is much better than the old-fashioned way of holding the iron close to the face. The latter test may result in an accident if the maid is suddenly startled.

Never secure clothes to the line by means of pins. See that you have a sufficiency of proper pegs, and finally, don't imagine that any amount of " Cleanser," no matter how much it may be advertised, will ever take the place of genuine rubbing, because it won't.

Bear in mind also that clothes, when ironed, should never be put away until they have been thoroughly aired; if this is omitted mildew is likely to result, and in addition, you run the risk of the maids, if careless, neglecting this precaution altogether. Have the lines, then, strung up in the kitchen, and *see for yourself* that all the clean things, but more especially the sheets, pillow slips, under-linen and flannels of every description are duly hung up, and receive their just need of airing, and also, it would be as well, never to allow them to be taken down until you have satisfied yourself that they really are thoroughly aired, since servants, especially those who are young and ignorant, are proverbially careless in this respect.

CHAPTER XII

ENTERTAINING

THE reader may perhaps feel inclined to ask *how* we managed to entertain at all upon means so limited as ours were.

Nevertheless, we did it, and it can be done by anyone similarly placed, who will take the trouble to plan things carefully.

To give a dinner party with the usual adjuncts, such as champagne, expensive liqueurs, etc., and with the table decorated by a fashionable florist, was, of course, out of our power.

Nevertheless, we often entertained half a dozen guests to a modest dinner, and that, too, without having to, in vulgar parlance, go short ourselves afterwards.

To begin with, if we served a *hors d'œuvre*, we used either one of the recipes I have already given you, or else smoked sardines (these latter cost four-pence-halfpenny a tin). Two were placed upon each plate, garnished with a few capers, and served with thinly-cut brown bread and butter, a single tin is quite sufficient for six or eight people, and we never exceeded this number at our parties, because, as it was quite out of the question that I could afford outside help, our two maids, who had to manage by themselves, would not have been able to cope with a greater number ; and then, too, as I could not exceed my weekly allowance, to entertain a dozen or more guests at a time was beyond our means.

For soup we invariably had a well-made vegetable purée, selecting one from the recipes I have already given, and enriching it for the occasion by the addition of a pennyworth of cream and the yolk of an egg.

For the first course we either had coquilles, or else a cream of fish served with an anchovy sauce, or sauce au fromage, or béchamel.

As a rule I did not give an entrée and joint both, but if the occasion was an important one, we generally had a dish of *petits vols au vent, or noisettes, and followed it up with a roast shoulder of mutton accompanied by chipped potatoes, red currant jelly, and any green well in season and consequently cheap.

This was followed in its turn by an entrée de legumes, say chou à la creme, or petit pois à la Française. And when fresh vegetables were dear, by butter beans à la Française. A sweet and a jelly, followed by a savoury and dessert concluded our repast.

In summer time I generally gave ices. We had invested in a cheap freezer, price 4s. 11d., and made an ordinary boiled custard, allowing one egg to each half pint of milk; flavoured it with essence of vanilla or lemon and froze it in the ordinary way. As the fullest directions are given with each freezer it is unnecessary for me to repeat them here.

* Both recipes given.

As regards the coffee, although we could not afford the finest mocha, I yet took care that our coffee was always well made, perfectly clear, and free from grounds and served *absolutely* boiling, and though we gave but 1s. a tin for it, I have often had people remark upon its excellence, and even ask me "where I got it."

As to wine, as we could not afford good port, burgundy, etc., we did without, and a cheap claret or hock had to suffice for our guests. We were fortunate enough to receive a case of sherry as a present, when we first started housekeeping, and so we were able to serve sherry in approved fashion with the first course, but in order to make it hold out we never touched it, except when we had people to dinner.

Upon other occasions, when we were alone, I drank water, and my husband contented himself with a glass or two of claret for which we paid 1s. a bottle.

You may perhaps wonder how I managed matters so as to enable my *two* maids to wait at table, so I will initiate you into the secret.

Penelope first, with my assistance as regards the more difficult dishes, cooked the dinner, and then we had a charwoman in for the evening, who dished up, and afterwards washed the dinner things and tidied up generally whilst Penelope and Mary were handing the coffee, etc., etc. For this service we paid her 1s. and gave her supper, but I only requisitioned her services upon very special occasions. At other times when we only had two or three people to dinner, Mary always managed by herself.

When first we were married, I told my husband that he need never hesitate to bring a man home to dinner unexpectedly. "There will always be a dainty dinner and a dainty table," I assured him, and I kept my promise.

Of course at first it was *not* easy, but gradually as I fell more into the way of things, I managed to cut and contrive so that there was always an ample meal and to spare for at least four people.

As to the decoration of the dinner table itself I managed thus :—

I went to a sale at a big "Art" shop, and there bought three cushion squares of art velvet which were priced at 1s. 6d. and 1s. 11d. each.

In addition I bought a long piece of white silk washing gauze, and these I utilized as centres, ringing the changes upon them and having a different one every evening. I always managed too, to save a few pence out of my housekeeping money for fresh flowers, but I was far too wise to let them present a skimpy appearance by arranging them in a wide mouthed vase capable of accommodating a dozen times their quantity.

I got a set, five in number, of creamy white china vases, taking care to select those with very tiny necks. In addition I got some small green specimen glasses, and these two sets I used alternately.

I got also a great bunch of silver honesty, and some dried fluffy grasses, and when flowers were very dear or unobtainable I used these.

At other times I kept the fluffy grass locked away, so that it should not get dusty and faded looking. I changed the water in the flower vases every day, and clipped the ends of the stalks, but .directly they showed even the slightest sign of withering off they went, for no table, let it bear ever so spotless a cloth, and be never so daintily laid, can possibly look even passably nice if adorned with withered flowers.

However, to revert to our original subject, that of entertaining.

Occasionally—for we received a great many invitations and went out a great deal, and were therefore in a measure compelled to return our friends' hospitality—we gave a small evening party.

As a rule we limited the number of our guests to thirty or thirty-five, sometimes even less, and we did not engage any waiters, first and foremost because we could not afford to do so, and secondly, because we both hated anything in the nature of false pretences and ostentation, and if our friends cared to come and see us, they had to take us and our little house in its everyday apparel, for we were both determined not to upset it and the servants by any attempts to turn things out of the course of their usual routine.

Of course anything in the nature of a sit-down supper was quite out of the question with our tiny dining-room and my tinier housekeeping allowance.

So the following is the menu I always adhered to :—

Sandwiches of (potted) Fish.
Chicken and Ham.   Strasbourg Meat.
Hot Soup in Cups.

Fish Salad.

Cold Beef.

Galantine.
Tartlets.   Salad.   Custards.

Jellies.   Blancmanges.
Jelly-cake.   Junket.

Tea.   Claret Cup.   Coffee.

The hot soup we made from the usual weekly stock. I got it as clear as I could, but I did not attempt to clarify it, as that would only have added to the expense.

However, I flavoured it thoroughly well, and saw that it was always boiling hot when sent up to the dining-room, and really the way people appreciated it was wonderful.

We had purées for the best part of the week afterwards, varying them every night, so as not to add to the butcher's bill for extra stock bones.

For the sandwiches I bought three pots of potted Strasbourg meat, salmon, and chicken and ham. These are put up by a well-known firm, and sold at a good grocer's price, 6½d. per pot. The three cost me just 1s. 7½d., and an extra pound of butter for the sandwiches, bread and butter, etc., another 1s.

For the fish salad, which was always a great

favourite and much appreciated, I bought a dried haddock, price 4d., a tin of smoked sardines, price 4½d., and in addition another portion of fish (for boiling) from my fishmonger, price 6d., and 1d. worth of picked shrimps; further I got 6d. worth of mixed salad from the greengrocer, and having done this, made the salad as follows :

Wash and dry the lettuce, etc., thoroughly, and tear it into pieces of a suitable size, place in a clean cold salad bowl, dust liberally with salt and pepper, grate a small shalot over, and dress with the oil from the smoked sardines. Add the haddock, first cooked, freed from skin and bone and flaked into pieces of a suitable size, the fish which should have been previously boiled allowed to get cold, freed from skin, bone, etc., and flaked into neat flakes, and finally the smoked sardines.

Mix lightly, using a silver fork for the purpose. Add two large tablespoonfuls of vinegar, mix again, garnish with the picked shrimps, and serve immediately.

For those of the men guests, whose appetites refused to be satisfied with sandwiches, there was always a joint of cold boiled brisket of beef; this was placed on the side table, together with plenty of thinly-cut bread and butter, mustard, etc., and a plentiful supply of knives and forks. They then had to carve it for themselves, and eat it as best as they could without sitting down, but somehow or other they always managed to accomplish this.

My butcher charged me 4½d. per lb. for brisket of beef, either fresh or salt, and the joint which generally weighed a little over five lbs., invariably came to about 2s. It was always accompanied by salad, and in winter, when salads are dear, we made this from equal portions of cold boiled butter beans, lentils, green peas, and cold sliced potatoes, a little grated onion, and oil and vinegar, in the proportion of two tablespoonfuls of the former, to one and a half of the latter, pepper and salt being added to taste. The galantine of veal we bought ready-made at the Stores, where, truffled and pistaché, it only cost us 1s. 6d.

We cut it into thin slices, as these could be more readily eaten with a fork only.

We always had four jellies, which we made by means of the popular packet jellies, selecting different flavours. These cost me 1s. 2d. (3½d. per packet). For the jelly-cake we scooped the inside out of a 6d. sponge cake (reserving the crumbs), fitted the inside with ribbon jelly, made by taking a little from each of the above jellies when in a liquid state, pouring this on to a large shallow dish, and when set, ripping it into ribbons by means of the point of a small teaspoon. Pour over the whole half a pint of boiled custard flavoured with vanilla. *Note.*—Use one egg to the half pint of milk, probable cost about 9d.

For the tartlets we bought a dozen empty patty cases, and filled these with jam; the little " tops " given with them, we treated thus : Scoop out the centres and fill with a chocolate mixture, place a bit of cream on top and serve.

The recipe for the chocolate will be found at page 97. We made a pint and a half of little custards, and in summer froze, and served them as ices. I reckoned the probable cost at 6d. We made a quart blancmange, using a quart of milk and half a packet of isinglass, reckoning flavouring, etc. I put down the cost of this at about 9d., and a large quart junket, which is always highly appreciated, cost another 5d. So that allowing 5d. for bread, 3d. for tea, 6d. for coffee, 8d. for milk, and 3d. for 2 lbs. of sugar, and 1s. 6d. for claret cup; the entire cost of our party was, say, 15s. 6d. at the outside. For the claret cup I allowed : One and a half bottles of claret 1s. 6d., two lemons, the juice of one, the other thinly sliced, 2d., two bottles of ginger beer 2d, two bottles soda water 3d., and sugar and a little brandy 1d. The deficiency we made up with ordinary water, adding the aërated waters at the last minute. Before you scoff at the idea of the common or garden ginger beer in claret cup, try it, and you will be surprised at the improvement it effects. As to the waiting we managed like this : The coffee was made beforehand, early in the afternoon, and then strained off, ready to be reheated when required ; the tea, however, being only made just before it was needed. Of the milk, I generally found a single quart sufficient as many people take black coffee, and a good many others prefer claret cup to anything else. I always had it sent up perfectly boiling, as this not only improves coffee enormously, but if the tea is getting at all cold, owing to standing, etc., it brings it up to the mark again.

The table we laid in this way : We drew it up to the sideboard end of the room, leaving just sufficient space for the maids to stand between the two. On the sideboard we placed the claret bowl, together with its attendant array of glasses.

The front part of the dining table, *i.e.* that towards the guests, we set out with flowers, creams, jellies, sandwiches, etc., etc., with here and there a pile of plates and plenty of forks and spoons. At the back, were the tea, coffee, and soup cups, with the sugar-basins, teaspoons, hot milk jugs, etc., and the urns containing the tea and coffee.

These, together with the claret cup, the maids served, but with this exception the guests waited upon themselves, the gentlemen attending to the ladies. Now and again, perhaps, when we had a bigger crowd than usual, our parties degenerated into rather a scramble, but they were none the less enjoyable on that account, and we rarely, if ever, had a refusal.

We had a monthly afternoon reception also, but at this I only gave brown and white bread and butter, hot tea-cakes (home-made these latter), and a little plum cake, tea and coffee. I took care, however, that the latter was always freshly made and quite hot, and that the bread and butter was daintly cut, and I reckoned out the cost of this monthly entertainment at, say about 4s. Half a lb. of tea 6d., three pints of milk 6d., two loaves of white bread 5d., one of brown 3d., coffee 3d., butter, $\frac{3}{4}$ of a lb. 9d., plum cake 1s., and home-made cakes, say 4d.

I generally contrived to save a little out of my housekeeping money every week, sometimes two or three shillings, sometimes less. This I religiously put away in a money-box, and the sum thus saved enabled us to give an occasional entertainment of the kind described above. But *until* I had the requisite sum saved up, we did not send out the invitations, as I knew well enough to do so would mean one or two things, running into debt, or going on short commons, both evils to be avoided by the wary housekeeper. The one thing I set my face against from the very first was, visitors to luncheon, because I knew what every housekeeper, who tries to manage on the same sum that I did, will speedily find out for herself, that a luncheon party means spending the money which ought to provide dinner, and therefore if you, my reader, wish to ask man or woman to share a meal with you, let that meal be dinner, not, most emphatically *not*, luncheon.

CHAPTER XIII

DRESS

ONE of the most vexed problems facing me was how to spend my dress allowance. Up to the time of my marriage everything had always been bought for me, and beyond choosing the colour and style of a dress, I had had little or nothing to do with garbing myself.

"Twenty-five pounds yearly, to buy everything with. Oh, I'm sure I can never do it," I thought despondently; and then I took my courage in both hands, and made up my mind that I would succeed in this, as I had succeeded in other things; that, moreover, I would be well-dressed into the bargain.

To this end I asked my husband to let me have my allowance half-yearly instead of quarterly, because to a woman with a small dress allowance there are sartorially but two seasons, summer and winter; autumn and spring don't count. He readily agreed to this, and then I proceeded to mentally map out my £12 10s.

Fortunately I had enough underlinen, white skirts, stockings, and fal-lals, generally to last quite a long time, but I knew that I must not let these get low, and therefore I decided to add to them, even before my stock needed replenishing.

"What could I wear to shop in?" was the next

question that presented itself, and to which I could find no satisfactory answer for some time.

Finally, I decided to invest in one of the half-guinea rough serge costumes advertised by a North of England firm.

I chose a dark navy blue, because this is one of the best colours for hard wear it is possible to select, and I wore it, coat and skirt, in conjunction with, in warm weather, a cotton, and in cold weather a flannel shirt and cuffs and collar.

In summer I discarded the coat, except on wet or chilly days, and wore my skirt with a cotton blouse or shirt. This gown I kept solely for out-of-door wear. For indoor wear in the morning I bought one of the serge skirts, sold by the same firm, for 5s. 6d., and wore that also in conjunction with shirts.

Apropos of the latter, I would have you note that I never invested in light-coloured or white shirts, etc. I always selected dark or butcher blue, with or without a white pin spot, or else bright scarlet, as these do not require such frequent washing as the pale pinks, blues, creams, and white one sees on every hand.

I also resolved, before indulging in any finery, to purchase all the absolutely necessary things *first*, and then to spend the residue, if any, on smart frocks, hats, etc. Boots and shoes claimed my attention next.

I got quite a smart pair of patents for half-a-guinea (these were for best), at a large shop, which claimed that the boots supplied by it fit more easily than those bought of other purveyors; and at the same establishment I got a pair of stout calf Oxford shoes for 8s. 11d., a pretty pair of court shoes, for evening wear, for 2s. 11d., and a very fair pair of brown Oxford shoes for 5s. 11d. Thus my shoe bill came to, roughly, about 28s. ; but as these shoes lasted considerably longer than a year, by dint of careful soling and heeling, etc., I decided that £1 2s. per year would be quite sufficient to satisfy my shoemaker.

I got three lengths of smart material for dresses, at a sale at one of the big Kensington shops, which cost me £1 10s., and I was fortunate enough to discover a little woman in our vicinity who fitted really well, and whose charge for making was only half-a-guinea !

I was careful to buy every scrap of lining, buttons, braid, dress preservers, etc., that she could possibly require, so that she was unable to charge me for extras, except a few pence for hooks and eyes, etc., and I bought some sateen at a sale which served for skirt and bodice linings.

These I was fortunate enough to obtain exceptionally cheap ; I think the whole bill only came to some 12s., so that those three dresses, and they were really smart little gowns, one of canvas, one of poplin, and one of a fancy check material, only cost me some three pound twelve or fourteen shillings altogether.

I gave 16s. 11d. for a really smart hat, and at quite a small shop I was lucky enough to pick up a little smartly trimmed toque, for second-best, for 8s. 11d., and these, with a sailor hat for morning wear, for which I paid 1s. 11d., constituted my millinery for the half-year.

We had been out so much that my evening dresses, two in number, were beginning to look sadly the worse for wear. One, a black bengaline, I renovated by means of an overdress of séquined net, which I picked up at a sale, skirt and material for bodice for a guinea.

Cheap satins, and cheap common silks of the pseudo fashionable kind I abhor, and as good ones were beyond my reach I determined to do without any, and had almost made up my mind to go in for an evening gown fashioned of nun's veiling, or some such inexpensive material, when at a sale I saw a dress length of surah, all silk, ticketed at 22s.; it was rose pink in colour, and perfectly fresh and unsoiled.

I•knew surah was slightly *démodé*, hence its low price, but I cared nothing for that, and promptly secured it.

Made up fashionably, and with touches of black chiffon here and there, it formed a really smart little gown.

Lining, extras, and making were another guinea, so that all told that frock cost me exactly £2 3s. *Moral.*—Buy a length of good material, even if it is slightly unfashionable, in preference to a cheap and shoddy article of later date.

On stockings, half-a-dozen pairs, also bought at a sale, I spent 6s.; a pair of corsets cost me another 5s. ; and for half-a-dozen pairs of gloves, also a bargain at one of the sales, I paid 11s. 6d. Thus my purchases for the first half-year came to about

£11, which, as you may see for yourself, didn't leave me with a very magnificent overplus in hand by way of private pocket money.

This, however, was the summer allowance (April), and when October came round I found that I had imperative need of a smart winter coat.

For every-day wear, on days when something warmer than my serge coat was needed, I had a reversible golf cape in a bronze and scarlet tartan which I picked up at an autumn sale for 12s. 6d.

For my smart winter coat, therefore, I went to a " sample shop," and secured a sacque in black velours de Nord, trimmed with a little jet, and a chiffon ruffle.

This cost me two guineas, and the material, making, lining, etc., for a warm winter best dress came to exactly £1 15s. A second best dress, material, making, etc., came to £1 5s. A guinea went in adding to my under-linen; 11s. 6d. for half-a-dozen pairs of gloves; 3s. 11d. for a moreen petticoat for every-day wear ; another guinea for a couple of winter hats ; 10s. 6d. for a pair of extra stout shoes ; 4s. 11d. for a pair of strong indoor shoes ; and another 4s. 11d. for a ready-made flannel shirt for wear with my coat and skirt. Up to now I had spent some £9 odd of my allowance, so I decided to save the remainder and expend it from time to time as I was obliged.

Now and again I had to spend a few odd shillings, too, for evening gloves, a little lace or trimming to furbish up one of my gowns, etc., but all extravagances that I possibly *could* do without, I did without.

Veils, for instance, run away with a by no means inconsiderable sum in a year, so I religiously avoided purchasing them. Then, too, I grew careful with pins and hairpins, and other small articles.

I took good care that my servants did not, as heretofore, make free with my needles, cottons, etc., etc. ; for it is in all these small ways that money is wasted, and can be saved. I never bought things for which I had not an immediate and definite use, and, above all, I never bought anything common. Better a stuff a little out of date, really good, than the most up-to-date of make-believe, thought I.

I grew to be careful, too, with my gowns, always wearing a dainty apron in the mornings when about my household duties. I never neglected that stitch in time which we are told saves nine of its own sort, and above all, though I was careful to have my gowns as well made as my means would allow, I never invested in anything ultra fashionable, for I knew that the markedly fashionable soon becomes the markedly unfashionable. I never invested in muslin gowns, since to look really well these need a visit to the laundress after being worn at the outside two or three times. It is only the heroine of a novel who can hope to look well in a badly got up muslin gown.

I never bought any gown in a so-called new colour, for these have an ugly way of dating themselves ; whilst one is always safe with dark blue, black, grey, and the more ordinary shades of brown and mauve, etc. In short, though it would tax my patience and the reader's to explain exactly how I spent every penny of my pin-money, I hope I have said sufficient to prove that one need not necessarily be a dowdy on a small dress allowance, and that as often as not good taste will go farther and fare better than a great deal of cash injudiciously expended. I always kept my eyes open for a bargain, but I never allowed myself to be tempted by bargains solely *because* they were bargains, and I can assure my readers that to the woman strong-minded enough to shop upon the lines I have laid down, the sales, genuine sales, at really reputable shops, spell sartorial salvation. Try it for yourself, and prove the truth of my words.

CHAPTER XIV

AMUSEMENTS

I AM a great believer in the truth of that maxim which tells us that " All work and no play makes Jack a dull boy." And of a surety if it makes Jack dull, it makes Jill still duller. For Jack has at least the distraction of going to and fro his office, the meeting with other business men, when the discussion is not quite every bit of it business ; whilst Jill, poor girl, has all the heat and burden of keeping house satisfactorily on a small income, in itself no inconsiderable strain, without all the petty annoyances it brings in its train. Alas, that the modern Jacks should think so little of it, and of all the many untiring efforts to make the household wheels run smoothly, when so very little grease in the shape of money is forthcoming !

However, for my part I had no intention of degenerating into dullness if I could possibly help it, so I suggested to my husband that we should form a common fund, and by saving all our odd pence, enable ourselves to go to the theatre, etc. occasionally.

He readily agreed to this, and really it is nothing short of wonderful how soon such odd pence do mount up, in our case so much so that on an average we managed to get to the theatre once a month at the very least. Of course dress seats, or even the upper boxes, were for us out of the question, but nevertheless we made ourselves very happy in the pit. Occasionally tickets for the dress circle or stalls were sent us from friends, and then indeed we felt luxurious ! But for the most part we were pittites and rather gloried in it than otherwise. We went to a good many concerts, too, 1s. seats always, and in summer, when the exhibitions were on, we generally managed to get there once a week, if we had not many engagements. Going to dances, etc., was, I admit, rather difficult work at first, because cabs, except upon very rare occasions, were out of the question, since they were quite beyond our means. But when by any chance we did indulge in a cab, I always pleaded that it might be to go, and not to come back in, unless the party or dance was to be a very late one, because if one goes in a cab one has at least the satisfaction of feeling perfectly fresh and unrumpled on arrival ; a thing one cannot hope for if travelling by bus or train ; while going back it really doesn't matter one way or another whether your dress, hair, etc., get crushed or not. I always wore a lace scarf by way of head gear. Nothing is so fatal to the well-being of a carefully dressed head as a hat and its attendant pins. " Skewers " my husband always calls them.

Fortunately for us a great many of our friends live within a walkable distance, so that even a bus was not always necessary. But when walking to a party I always wore goloshes over my evening shoes, as this, besides minimizing the risks of cold, saves the shoes and prevents them getting dusty.

For an evening cloak I had got my " little woman " to fashion me in a long Empire coat of black surah silk. This was made so that, while amply covering my dress, it just cleared the ground ; it was lined with scarlet flannelette, and though warm and light, and looking essentially smart, its total cost only stood, roughly, at about £1 17s. 6d. thus : Twelve yards of black Surah silk, 1s. 11½d. per yard, £1 3s. 6d. ; twelve yards scarlet flannelette 3¾d. yard, 3s. 9d. ; making, 7s. 6d. ; extras, ribbon, chiffon, etc., 2s. 6d.

It was equally suitable for winter or summer wear, but I admit it was rather hot in summer. And while it was sufficiently quiet to pass unnoticed in bus or train, yet it looked quite smart enough for the stalls of a theatre. By the way I had the flannelette lining made detachable, so that when soiled it could be removed, washed, and put back again.

To go back to our amusements, however. Neither of us cycled, and, as a matter of fact, could not at that time have afforded the money necessary to purchase a cycle apiece, but we often took short trips by train, up river, and had tea in quaint little inns, when one or other of us had got a hoard saved. So that you see even on £300 a year one need not forego all pleasures if one is really clever enough to take them economically.

CHAPTER XV

THE ANNUAL HOLIDAY

ALL the rest of our world were about to take a trip to seaside or country, but for us it seemed very much as if the expense of such a jaunt would be beyond us, and in fact we had grown almost resigned to spending August and September in town, when I saw the following advertisement in one of the daily papers : " Pretty furnished cottage to be let. Four bedrooms, sitting-room and kitchen, bracing locality, rent 10s. weekly." I gasped with mingled delight and astonishment. After all, then, we needn't go without a holiday; who would ever have thought that a cottage and a furnished one at that, could be had so cheaply.

I am wiser now, and for the reader's benefit let me state that there are hundreds such to be had every holiday season, in quaint unfrequented little places, whose rentals range from 10s. to £1 per week, the sole drawback to them lying in the fact that they are as a rule generally situated from a mile to two or three miles distant from a railway station, and of course always in out-of-the-way and unfashionable districts.

However, to go on. We ran down for the day to the quaint little village mentioned in the advertisement, and were so charmed with the cottage and its surroundings, that we straightway took it for six weeks. Cutlery and plate by the way were actually included in the 10s. And then a happy thought struck me. What a pity to leave two out of those four bedrooms lying empty, because of course we only needed one for ourselves and one for the two servants. So I asked a couple of friends who I happened to know were, like ourselves, none too well off, if they would care to join us on our holiday, telling them if they would pay me £1 per week, I could give them board, lodging, everything in fact but washing in return.

Fortunately for us they accepted with celerity, and a very jolly time we had between us. For the benefit of such of my readers who may care to copy our example, I will explain how we managed.

Our own house was the first thing to be thought of, for we meant to take the two servants with us. Therefore after taking down every scrap in the shape of hangings, etc., we packed them carefully away in cupboards and drawers with plenty of carbon to keep out the moths. The contents of the glass and china and linen cupboards were neatly arranged and then locked. All ornaments of every description were put away. We happened to have very little upholstered furniture of any sort, but for such as there was I made loose covers of yellow calico—it cost me $1\frac{3}{4}$d. a yard this latter— and tied them on securely. Ornaments of every description I put under lock and key, and our modest store of silver and electro-plate we packed in a box—with a big lump of camphor to prevent it from tarnishing—and sent it down to my husband's office. The carpets were thoroughly swept, sprinkled with carbon, and then rolled up to await our return, the rugs, etc., being treated in the same way.

All this, I will admit, necessitated a good deal of hard work, and a certain amount of discomfort prior to our departure from town, but nevertheless I persevered because I knew that on our return instead of having to face a vast amount of the accumulated dust and dirt of weeks on carpets, rugs, ornaments, curtains, hangings, etc., I should find all these fresh and clean, and that the actual sweeping and scrubbing necessary would take but a day or two at the outside.

Then when we were ready to start, we carefully secured every door and window, and having tipped the local policeman who had but just come on night duty for the month, and promising him another tip on our return if he would keep a sharp look-out upon the house during our absence, we set off with light hearts.

I had determined to take the servants with me, for two very good and solid reasons. First, on the score of economy, because their board wages at the very lowest computation would come to £1 a week, 10s. each, and this for six weeks meant no less than £6 and secondly, because I thought they were over young to be left in entire charge of a house such as ours, and that they would be safer under my own eye.

In this my husband agreed with me, so we made up our minds to run the risk of burglars, and up to now have never had to regret our rashness in doing so.

Having decided this point, the next thing to engage my attention was the commissariat. I knew that in a small country village such as we were going to, groceries in addition to being very dear would most probably be of inferior quality, and I therefore determined to take with me sufficient stores to last us the six weeks. I reckoned out the quantities per head of tea, sugar, coffee, etc., which we should require, and as we were starting on a Saturday I expended the best part of my week's allowance in provisions which I had packed and took with me. In addition I took also a joint for the next day's dinner, and sufficient vegetables to see us over a day or two until I could look round and decide how and where I could shop. All these things were packed together in a cheap trunk, and went with the rest of the luggage. I append a list of the things necessary for the reader's benefit, together with prices.

6 lbs. of tea, 1s. a lb., 6s. 36 lbs. of 1½d. lump sugar, 4s. 6d. 6 lbs. of cooking sugar, 1½d. lb., 9d. 6 1-lb. tins of coffee, 6s. 2 lbs. of chocolate powder, 8d. lb., 1s. 4d. Two tins of Swiss milk, 4½d. tin, 9d. 1 dozen pint packets of jelly powders, 3s. 9d. 6 lb. 1½d. rice, 9d. 2 lb. of pearl barley, 4d. 6 lb. of butter beans, 1s. 4d. packet of salt. 6d. tin of mustard. Bottle of oil, 6d. Bottle of vinegar, 6d. 7-lb. jar of cooking jam, 1s. 6d. 7-lb. jar of marmalade, 1s. 4d. Large tin of golden syrup, 10d. 2 lb. tapioca, 6d. 2 lb. sago, 6d. 4 lb. lunch biscuits, 2½d. lb., 10d. Dutch cheese (whole), 2s.

A packet of dessicated soup, 1s. Pepper and the spice box I took from home.

The total, together with the joint and vegetables and some butter, came to just £2.

Our friends insisted upon paying me in advance and this made catering easier.

Upon arrival, while we unpacked and washed, etc., the servants got a high tea ready.

I had taken down some cold meat left from the previous day's dinner, and of course as the stores had only to be opened they had everything at hand.

After tea we set off on a voyage of exploration, and upon enquiring at a neighbouring cottage, I learnt that milk and bread, butter and eggs, could all be obtained either at an adjacent farm or at the village shop (I decided upon the farm instanter), and that a butcher's cart from the nearest town three miles away, called every day with meat and poultry.

Vegetables were to be had either at the post-office, which was also the local stores, drapers, everything in fact, or at the above-mentioned farm.

So housekeeping was made comparatively easy, and I felt at liberty to enjoy myself. The better to further this, and to enable Penelope to get in a little holiday on her own account, I decided to have a plain early dinner, and a cold supper.

With this end in view, I went in largely for beef steak puddings, stews, Irish stews, etc., with now and again a joint of either roast mutton or beef, one of the latter always on Sundays, and an occasional piece of boiled brisket with carrots, turnips, and suet dumplings by way of accompaniment.

In short we went in for the more solid side of English cookery, as opposed to the *cuisine bourgeoise* we practised in town, and we found the change for the time being both healthful and pleasant.

As I already had the stores to start with, I found that the two pounds we received from our boarders, as we called them, just paid the housekeeping expenses comfortably, and out of our own pockets we only had the rent to pay, so that actually during the whole of our holiday we were saving money.

We found out that the village postmaster had a cart to let out for which he charged the modest sum of 1s. 6d. an hour, so on three days a week we hired this for two or three hours, and made excursions to the neighbouring villages. Sometimes we took a tea basket, and at others, when the funds were rather more plentiful, we had tea at an inn. The cost of hiring the cart we divided between us.

On other days we went for picnics or lazied about the garden (it actually had a garden that cottage), doing nothing.

The nearest town boasted a circulating library, " books lent 2d. per volume " kind of thing, and we became patrons of this, so that when there was nothing else to do one could always walk in to—— and change the books.

We made friends with the family who had taken the cottage adjoining ours. It was, I believe, slightly higher rented, anyway it boasted a piano, and we used to go in and have musical evenings.

Altogether, a jollier holiday than ours proved to be, it would, I think, be difficult to imagine, and the good that it did us was simply inestimable. Just one word more *re* the commissariat.

We did not, except on Sundays, have meat for supper as a regular thing. For preference we indulged in Spanish onions, cheese, eggs, etc., but occasionally we had a hash, made from the remains of the cold meat when there was not enough left to provide dinner for the following day, and we always had a hot substantial pudding.

As we had supper at seven-thirty and did not go to bed till half-past ten, this was really not so indigestible as it sounds.

For breakfast, we had, sometimes, eggs and bacon, sometimes eggs alone, and occasionally when fish was obtainable, kippers or dried haddock. Once or twice I got a little hock of country bacon cheaply, and this, after it had figured hot, with boiled greens at our early dinner, reappeared as a breakfast dish.

Lettuce, watercress, or green stuff of one kind or another we always had; together with a dish of some sort of fruit, for preference baked apples when we could get them, but as a rule fruit in small villages, such as the one I have been describing, is very cheap, more especially in the counties of Kent, Devonshire, Somersetshire, and Berkshire, and I believe, in Cornwall, although I have had no practical experience of the latter county.

Finally, I would advise any of my readers who may contemplate a holiday upon similar lines to ours, to keep their eyes open as the holiday season approaches, and to have a sharp look out on the advertisement columns of one or other of the daily papers.

If you don't see just what you want advertised, put an advertisement in yourself, and it is pretty certain to bring you a host of replies.

Not alone inland are cottages such as I have described to be had, there are numbers of the like at little unfrequented seaside places, sans a pier and band perhaps, but to the tired, jaded worker who doesn't want to change her dress some half dozen times a day, all the more acceptable on that account. The rents asked are as a rule slightly higher at the seaside than inland, but the excess is so very trifling that it will be found well worth your while to pay it if sea air suits you better than country.

This year, for example, I went to look over a thoroughly well-furnished and comfortable house at Pevensey Bay, for which only 30s. weekly was *asked*. And when 30s. is *asked*, as a pretty general thing 25s. will be accepted, especially if the "let" is to be a good one of six or eight weeks' duration. The house just referred to had, for example, five thoroughly well-furnished bedrooms, a drawing and dining-room, a neat little kitchen with a really capable modern range, and all the latest sanitary improvements. Moreover, it was situated right facing the beach, the only drawback being so far as I could see, that it was some two and a half miles distant from the nearest railway station. In the same village were to be had smaller houses at rentals of from one pound a week and upwards.

And to take a leap from Sussex to Devonshire, a friend of mine has just vacated a cottage in Seaton, that loveliest of all fishing villages, for which she has only paid 10s. weekly during August and September. And, moreover, it was well and completely furnished, having not only plate and linen, but a piano into the bargain! Other houses in the same village boasting, some of them, five bedrooms, were to be had for a modest £1 per week. One word of advice, though, I would give you. If possible select a locality where you will be able to run down and inspect your house before finally taking it. The article known "as a pig in a poke " is one to be avoided by the wary, and a holiday spent in unlovely surroundings is not likely to result in much good to either mind or body. Therefore beware of the bogus "country " cottage, and inspect your bargain before you—rent it. For the rest I hope I have said enough to prove to you that even on £300 a-year it is not necessary to forego one's annual holiday if one goes wisely about the taking thereof.

CHAPTER XVI

THE FAMILY MEDICINE CHEST

THE importance of keeping in good health is a thing which cannot be over-rated, and more especially is this the case with regard to the mistress of a household. Ill-health spells doctor's bills, and all their attendant ills, and to the possessors of a very limited income a heavy doctor's bill is something to be avoided if possible. Now, it is a good deal easier to get out of health than it is to get well again. But, although it sounds rather an unfeeling sort of thing to put in cold black and white, the average woman with indifferent health has often only herself to thank for it.

Take the daily meals, for instance.

Perhaps she eats a fairly good breakfast to start with, but, once the husband is safely out of the house, of what does her luncheon too often consist? Why, of a cup of overstrong tea and a piece of bread and butter of wafer-like thinness, or else, what is even worse, an indigestible cream bun or cake. This repast is repeated at five o'clock under the title of afternoon tea, and supposing that breakfast was at 8.30 or nine in the morning, and dinner is at 7.30 in the evening, there is thus an interim of eleven hours between the two meals.

Now, I put it to your common sense, my reader, can any woman in her senses expect to keep in even fairly good health under such adverse conditions? When she goes to town for a day's shopping the same thing occurs; no matter how faint with hunger she may be she usually lunches? at a tea-shop off a sweet cake and a cup of tea or coffee. And then she wonders that she feels ill and weak, depressed and out of sorts.

Now, small means, which are invariably urged as an excuse for this sort of thing, is really no excuse at all.

There are now plenty of restaurants where—if your means will not permit you to indulge in a meat luncheon—a plateful of good Scotch broth and a roll can be obtained for sevenpence. Only a single penny more than your " tea meal " would cost, you see, and where, if you can afford it, for 1s. 6d. you can get a lunch consisting of meat, two vegetables, bread and pudding.

At home a luncheon such as I have before described, consisting of plenty of good soup and followed by a substantial pudding, need add nothing to the household bills, if you go the right way to work about it, giving your butcher a standing order for sixpennyworth (twelve pounds) of bones, and having the stock made weekly as I advised in a previous chapter.

For myself, I had seen so much of what I felt were the ill effects resulting from a long-continued course of tea lunches among my young married women friends, that I determined, when once I set up house, never to follow their example, and I didn't.

I confess a meal eaten in solitude isn't particularly

enlivening just at first, especially to a girl who may have but recently come from a big jolly circle of brothers and sisters. But this dislike to eating alone, which is after all but a purely sentimental one, soon passes away, and sentiment is but a poor thing unless it is backed up by good health.

As a rule it is the married women without children who are the greatest sinners in this respect. Once the little ones come, and the one o'clock luncheon becomes a regular institution all is well, unless, as is too often the case, a woman has already done herself incalculable injury by her previous foolish abstinence.

If you think I am in any way overstating the case or exaggerating, ask your medical man, and you will find that he will confirm what I say up to the hilt.

For this reason, when I started housekeeping, I instituted a regular solid, but not heavy, lunch, both for myself and the servants, and I am bound to say I am all the better for it, although at first I didn't like eating alone, any more than anyone else.

Another mistake, too frequently made by young wives with respect to their own health, is this: When, as in the spring for instance, they feel run down and generally debilitated, they wait on and on, hoping it "will pass off," instead of, as they should do, going straight to a doctor at once. A tonic taken in time will often save loads of chemist's stuff, and the single five shillings which that visit would cost you, many and many a long bill and hour of ill-health.

But don't, I beg of you, go to the other extreme and start "quacking" yourself. You are bound to regret it if you do, either in pocket or in health, more probably in both. You see, one never knows exactly what those wonderful advertised medicines are composed of. It may be nothing more harmful than sugar and water, in which case only the pocket suffers, but then there is always the chance that the special nostrum you have chosen contains the very drug which would be most harmful to you.

For myself, when I feel out of sorts, I consult a medical man, and I would advise you to do the same. It is cheaper in the long run, believe me, and many and many an attack of nervous breakdown has been saved before this by the administration of a simple timely tonic.

Then again as regards the health of your household, prevention is also better than cure. A thoroughly clean house cannot be an altogether unhealthy house, but no matter how clean the house itself may be, if the sinks, lavatories, etc., are not kept well flushed and sweet, especially in hot weather, illness may result therefrom.

Too much importance also cannot be attached to keeping the dust-bin in good order, and having it emptied at regular intervals. The following is the plan I adopted and carried out, whether it was needed or not, winter and summer alike : Once a week, every sink, lavatory, etc., in the house was well flushed with chloride of lime water, hot water *bien entendu*, being used for the purpose.

The reason for this is, I hope, obvious ; for instance, in the case of the sink pipe becoming in danger of being stopped with greasy accumulations, as the hot water softens and disperses these.

So too with the ordinary drains; give them first a thorough flushing with hot and *then* a final one with as much cold water as you like.

The hot will cleanse away all impurities, and leave the pipes in a much sweeter and cleaner condition than any amount of cold water could possibly do. As a great many people strongly object to the smell of chloride of lime, and are apt to fancy something is wrong with the drains in a house where it is used, this flushing should be done the very first thing in the morning, as soon as the water in the boiler is hot enough to permit of its being used for the purpose. If this plan is pursued by the time ordinary callers commence making their appearance, all odour will have vanished completely, especially if after the chloride water has been poured down the drains are well flushed, as I advised, with the cold.

With regard to the dust-bin, you should never allow vegetable refuse of any sort to be thrown into this, more particularly if the dust-bin happens to be in close proximity to the kitchen or living rooms.

All scraps of vegetable refuse, potato peelings, etc., should be burnt as soon as possible. Egg shells, however, which are productive of such an unpleasant smell when being burnt, may be thrown into the dust-bin with perfect safety, so long as none of the egg remains adhering to the shell. Fish bones, and indeed bones of every description, should also be burnt. The smell from these can be obviated if a little cedar powder be thrown on the top of the stove during the process. This can be obtained at any of the big Stores, or at any grocers, and is very inexpensive, costing but 4½d. for a large sized tin. It is useful too in a variety of the same ways. *Par exemple*, when greens are being boiled—and to cook greens properly the lid of the saucepan should always be off during the cooking operations; if a little is thrown on the top of the stove, only the pleasant odour of the burnt cedar dust will be perceptible through the house instead of that too pungent *bouquet de choufleur*, or *chou*, as the case may be, when fish is in process of frying or boiling, or when onions or garlic is being cooked.

Indeed, to my mind, no mistress of a small household should be without this really invaluable stuff. I say small, advisedly, because it is in small households that greens and such things do make their presence felt most acutely.

But to go on.

Another point it behoves you to be careful over is in the quality of the provisions you buy. Many people, for instance, may cross swords, or wish to do so with me, because I advocate the purchase of cheap foods, and more especially New Zealand and American meat in place of Scotch mutton and English or Scotch beef. So here let me claim for myself, that, though I plead the cause of that which is cheap, it must needs be good also, since I am a sworn foe of that which is cheap and nasty in any shape or form.

Better by far a good wholesome joint of New Zealand mutton or prime American beef than a shoulder or sirloin of the "best English," slightly off colour and reduced in price in consequence, and yet I have known people who would turn up their noses with the utmost contempt at the first, buy the second with avidity, simply and solely *because it was English*, and consider they have got a great bargain!

Comment of course is superfluous, but when one thinks of the actual tangible danger attendant on buying meat which is even in the slightest degree tainted, one wonders at their temerity.

For this reason too, pork, unless you can afford to buy it at a shop above suspicion, which in plain language means paying a fair price for it, should be avoided. *Never buy cheap pork*, no matter how fond you may be of that delicacy. It is not safe.

Never buy unsound fruit or vegetables, even though the unsoundness consist of but the tiniest speck here and there.

Never buy, and certainly never *cook* fish which you even suspect to be tainted, no matter how slightly, and above all, don't buy cheap margarine for cooking. Save the dripping from the joints, and clarify that as I have before advised; it is a far more satisfactory frying medium.

Don't be tempted into buying this or that article of food just because at the moment it happens to be "so cheap," pause and consider whether you can use it up at once, and if not, steel your heart against temptation and avoid it; that is true economy, whereas if you buy without actually needing, it may grow stale before it is cooked, and stale food of all sorts, with the one exception of bread, is bad for the health of both you and yours.

All these are small things, and of the order known as trifles, of this I am well aware, nevertheless the observance of them goes far towards keeping a household in good health.

I am not, as you will have gathered, an advocate for amateur doctoring, but there are, I consider, some few remedies which every mistress of a household should possess, locked away for safety, but conveniently to hand when required. Amongst these should be a bottle of pure olive oil for burns, etc., and a small bottle of carron oil—the latter is made by mixing linseed oil and limewater in equal proportions, and is useful as a remedy for scalds or burns. A bottle of liquorice powder for use as an aperient, and another bottle of Epsom salts, for use when something rather more drastic is required. A bottle of embrocation for use for strained muscles, sprains, a slight attack of rheumatism, etc. A bottle of camphorated oil for rubbing into the chest for colds, etc., a bottle of citrate of magnesia, useful when a cooling draught is required, a packet of mustard leaves, a packet of porous plasters, a shilling bottle of diarrhœa mixture, this you should never be without, especially in the hot weather, and above all a bottle of brandy. This latter should be kept in the medicine chest, and should never be used on any pretext save that of illness. No matter whether your own stock of brandy runs out or not, you should never encroach upon the medicine brandy— which, by the way, should be the best your means will permit you to buy—upon any pretext whatever. By pursuing this simple plan you will be able to make sure of always having brandy in the house, a thing you could not otherwise do, if you keep it with the ordinary stock of wines, spirits, etc., and allow it to be used haphazard.

Thus far, in my opinion, your stock of home medicines go, but no farther, for as I have said before, amateur doctoring is a thing to be avoided. Still in this connection it is as well to bear in mind the trite and true old proverb that "Prevention is better than cure," and therefore to do everything in your power by keeping your house in a clean and sanitary condition to lessen the need for a doctor's services.

CHAPTER XVII

KEEPING UP APPEARANCES

KEEPING up appearances! The words have perhaps, to the uninitiated, rather a terrifying sound, implying all sorts of shifts and struggles. A smiling face to the world, an aching heart and a bare cupboard at home ; but really and truly if if one only goes sensibly to work, keeping up appearances need mean nothing of the sort. To my mind the phrase should mean making the best the very best of what one has, and not pretending to be what one is *not*, and to possess that which one lacks.

There is a good and a bad side to keeping up appearances as there is to most things in this world, and all honour should be done to the wife and house mistress who extract the greatest comfort and daintiness out of a small income. Take those three most important things of any in daily life— food, servants, and dress.

It costs no more, nay, rather less, to have dainty well served meals, than it does to make shift—how I hate that term—with a pound of cooked beef and a bottle of indigestible pickles, half a pound of cheese, and a loaf of new bread from an adjacent ham and beef shop. It costs no more, I say, no, not one whit, but what it *does* call for is untiring and increasing energy on the part of the housewife.

It means taking pains and using infinite patience when training your raw cook general at £10 a-year, if you want to turn her into a good capable, economical cook.

It means teaching, teaching, teaching, every time you come in contact with your little handmaiden at 2s. or 2s. 6d. a week if you would turn her into a neat-handed house-parlourmaid. But it can be done. Oh, yes, and easily done, if you will but take the trouble to do it, as I have proved in my own case.

The make-shift meal above referred to will cost you—Beef, one pound, 1s. 6d.; pickles, 6d.; cheese, 4d.; bread, 3d.; butter, 2d.; total, 2s. 9d., whilst a dainty meal consisting of soup, French stewed steak, potatoes, *chou à la creme*, and golden toast need only cost you exactly the same sum, perhaps less. Twopennyworth of bones, a carrot, an onion, and a little salt will furnish the soup if you follow the recipe I have already given in one of the opening chapters.

A pound and a half of eightpenny steak will cost you 1s., carrots, onions, turnips, garlic, dripping for frying, and a pinch of flavouring, say another 3d.; four pound of potatoes, 2d., say 1s. 5d. A cabbage, 2d., an onion, and a pennyworth of cream for the entrée, say 3½d. For the golden toast : cut some slices of stale bread and soak them in a little sweetened milk flavoured with vanilla. Dip in egg and bread crumb and fry in deep fat, take out quickly, drain carefully, spread each with a little apricot jam and serve at once. Total cost perhaps 4d., certainly not more. Allow another 2d. for bread, and the totàl cost of your dainty meal which, allowing quarter pound of meat per head, should be sufficient for five people, is but 2s. 5d. So that you actually *save* over the transaction, and if you expend that 4d. in fruit you have dessert into the bargain!

Then as to laying the table daintily—

One or two practical lessons from her mistress are all that is needed to teach even the rawest girl to set a table properly, and it is not one whit more trouble to place the things properly than it is to fling them on anyhow. A dainty table centre need cost but a few pence, and if care is taken of it, and it is properly folded, it will last for quite an indefinite time.

A threepenny or sixpenny worth of flowers in small specimen glasses if arranged with taste will have quite as good an effect as half a guinea's worth of costly blooms.

A small income is no excuse for a soiled table-cloth, and if the latter is used carefully, and folded in the same creases as those in which it arrived home from the laundry, even with a very limited stock of table linen at command the table should always look spotless : well polished glass and clean shining plate is within the reach of everybody who possesses a few wine glasses and tumblers, and the necessary knives, spoons and forks. That the latter are but electro-plated, and perhaps of an inferior quality at that, is no excuse for a lack of lustre, and that your glass is but blown and not cut, no excuse for its being sent to table in the condition known as " smeary."

Now, young and untrained servants are proverbially careless in this respect, as I found to my cost
when first I started housekeeping, but the one and,
indeed, the only way to cure them of this is to send
the article, whatever it may be, back to the kitchen
then and there to be washed and repolished, no
matter whether you have to wait for it or not. This
is the plan I always adopted, and I have proved
from experience that, after a few times, it has a
most salutary effect.

For the final polish, both for glass and plate, a
chamois leather should always be used, as a cloth
is apt to leave bits of fluff on the article in question;
and even when it does not do so, quite the same
brilliancy as the chamois gives is never obtainable.

However, to return to the subject of the servants
themselves. A small income is no more excuse for
a dirty, slovenly servant, than it is for any of the
things above quoted. The wages of a clean, neat
girl are not higher than those of a slattern, and it
won't cost you a single penny more to feed her
either.

A clean, careful girl should be able to make three
afternoon aprons, and one or, at the outside, two
smart caps last her a week at least, and if she
cannot do so and, moreover, always keep herself
smart and tidy, it is no use your keeping her, if
you wish to keep up appearances too. Even in
working hours she can always be presentable if
she goes the right way to work.

For myself, I don't allow my servants to wear
pale hued print gowns, as after the first time of
wearing, and working in, these are invariably unfit

to answer the door in. Choose dark blue print, either plain or with a tiny white spot, or else plain dark grey linen. Both these are obtainable at any good draper's for 5¾d. or 6¾d. a yard, and with care they will both wear a month without requiring a visit to the laundress; and, believe me, nothing is so detrimental to the smart appearance of a house as a dirty or semi-dirty and wholly untidy maid. Therefore, if you get one, make a clean sweep of her, unless she will consent to mend her ways instanter. For in keeping up appearances it is, you must must bear in mind, the little things that count. Take afternoon tea, for instance. When you have a caller, you may not, perhaps, be able to afford tennis or polo cake or the latest thing in sweet biscuits, but the bread and butter can be daintily cut and rolled, the tea well and freshly made, and the hot water jug filled with absolutely boiling water; the tea tray, even though it may lack silver, can be daintily set, and if the maid who carries it in is also smart, clean, and wholesome to look at, depend upon it the cake will never be missed, of that you may rest assured.

So, too, with the dinners, and the waiting at dinner. You may not be able to afford bisques, salmon and whitebait, game and poultry, pineapples and black grapes, but if your simple purée is hot, the grilled herrings and mustard sauce cooked to a turn, and your stewed steak or blanquette de veau hot and nicely seasoned, your golden toast crisp and well drained, and if, moreover, all these things are served as they should be, you will never miss luxuries, even though your Hebe's wages are but a single half-crown a week, and you have trained her yourself.

And where the husband is out all day long at his office or business, the training is, or should be, so very, very easy. I grant you if the private house is also the professional one, that then your path is not so easy, because a well and thoroughly trained parlourmaid is an absolute necessity. I daresay a volume could be written of the friends offended, and the business lost, through the all-unconscious rudeness of an ignorant and untrained maid, but then I am not writing of such households as these, but of one where the master is away all day, and the wife and house mistress is consequently left to her own devices.

For such an one to have ill-trained and careless servants is nothing less than disgraceful.

But when training a young girl, no matter how stupid she may be, you must take care not to lose your temper. Force yourself to be gentle, no matter how distasteful the effort may be, for stupid girls can be very irritating, as I know from prolonged experience. Explain, if need be, over and over, aye, and over again, until she does understand what you mean and can put it into practice, and you will, I think, be surprised to find how even the dullest fifteen-year-old will expand and improve under this treatment. Never allow a fault, either in waiting, answering the door, speaking, etc., no matter how slight it may be, to pass unchecked and uncorrected, because little faults are apt to grow into big ones, and to crop up and humiliate you, just when you would wish that Hebe should be on her very best behaviour. Don't let her "forget her cap"—they will all do this, young ignorant girls, if you give them half a chance—or to bring letters, telegrams, change, etc., on a waiter; and, above all, never allow any familiarity with your parlourmaid, it is bound to turn into contempt sooner or later if you do. With the cook you should be equally careful, though if you wish to get her to study your interests you must, as I have said before, endeavour, to a certain extent, to make her a friend, and get her to take something more than that frigid impersonal interest which is the attitude of the average maid towards that natural enemy, her mistress. If all these little items, which, though small in themselves, go to make up the grand total of daily comfort or discomfort, are studied as they should be, keeping up appearances need not prove such a difficult thing after all.

Of course, in the foregoing pages I have only been considering the case of those without little children, for where there are babies, real babies, the difficulty is of course enormously increased, since a nurse, or rather a nurse girl of some sort or another is an absolute necessity, and this means another mouth to feed, not that this is in itself an insuperable obstacle, because in my own experience I have found that which will feed two servants will feed three, as there is always that "little over" which comes in, but there is the question of the extra washing and the extra wages, which, though perhaps small in themselves, make a big inroad when the total income only averages £300 a year.

One word of advice I should like to give to any young and inexperienced mother who may be among my readers.

If you can't by hook or by crook afford a thoroughly trained and experienced nurse for your baby, don't, whatever you do, allow a young nurse to have " entire charge " as it is called, for if you do the chances are 1,000 to 1 that you will sooner or later rue it, no matter how " kind-hearted " and fond of the child she may be. You must bear in mind that no amount of kindheartedness or affection can possibly make up for lack of experience, and if your means will only permit you to afford a young girl for nurse, the child should sleep in your room at least until it can speak, or if you *must* have it sleep with the nurse, then her room should lead out directly of yours. Don't trust even the " opposite landing," and don't, no matter how much you may feel inclined to do so, leave a baby in a young girl's charge for an entire day; when a child is able to walk and talk, the case is different, then any strong, healthy young girl—for preference a country girl should always be chosen—is quite capable of looking after it and doing all that is required, but with a baby all the future health and even sanity depends on the nurse, and therefore a mother who cannot afford an experienced woman as nurse, should be *herself* the nurse.

All this I know savours a little of over caution, but after all it is over and not under caution which gives the best results in the long run. So I for one am all in favour of over-caution. But to go on once more. To make the keeping up of appearances absolutely successful you must be able to pay your way, and though paying your way may leave you with but a single halfpenny overplus in hand. If you *have* that halfpenny you may claim that you have succeeded. For this reason I say, as I have said before, don't have any weekly bills, or, for the matter of that, any bills at all. Pay for everything just as you have it, and in the long run you will find that by so doing you are the gainer both in purse and peace of mind.

For one thing, by paying cash you do away with even the possibility of over-charging, and for another, you have the inestimable comfort of feeling and knowing that every mouthful you eat and every stitch you wear is paid for, and keeping up appearances under these conditions should be easy. I know that I have found them so.

CHAPTER XVIII

SUCCESS

THE truth of the old adage that "nothing succeeds like success" was amply exemplified in our case. For at the end of a few months, not only had I succeeded in "keeping up appearances," but my two raw maids had become transformed the one into a very tolerable cook, the other into a really deft waitress. "Oh!" I fancy I can hear some sceptical reader say, "They must have been exceptionally sharp and clever girls to start with." Now as a matter of honest fact they were nothing of the sort, my little parlourmaid, in particular being rather stupid, and prone to make somewhat ridiculous mistakes at first than otherwise, but the method I adopted, would, I flatter myself, have turned even coarser material than I had to deal with to advantage.

I was unstinting too, with my praise, and when I had to find fault, I did so at the time pretty forcibly, or as my husband put it, "let them have it hot." Yet once I *had* finished my lecture, or scolding, call it which you will, I never referred to the subject again. The very greatest mistake a mistress can make is to "nag," and it is safe to say a nagging mistress *never* has good servants. For one thing the latter know that do what they will, the nagging goes on just the same, and for another, they rapidly grow hardened, and in course of time take no more notice of reproof, merited or unmerited, than they would of a dog barking in the street. So don't nag, young housewives, if you want your domestic path to be one of peace and (comparative) freedom from worry. But to go on. Not only was I successful with the servants, but I had actually managed to save a few shillings, just over a pound, to be exact, and so far as the household was concerned, we did not owe a farthing to anybody. (It is useless to expect a man not to owe his tailor's bill, I have found this out from long experience. They seem to think that clothes for which they pay cash won't fit.) Moreover, I did not owe a dressmaker's bill either, because I made it a rule never, no matter how much I might feel tempted to do so, to owe for more than one dress at a time, and as regards all other items appertaining to the wardrobe, why I paid for them then and there as soon as I had chosen them. Our little parties, modest as they were, had been great successes also ; we had made new friends, many of whom eventually found their way to my husband as clients, and they in turn had recommended others, so that thus his business was continually upon the increase. So here you see was *one* valuable result of keeping up appearances. Then too, knowing as he did, that a dainty well-cooked meal was always awaiting him, he had several times brought home a business friend to dinner, and to this he ascribed more than one stroke of good luck which had befallen us. Men are in a much more amenable mood after a good meal, let it be never so simple so long as it is cooked to perfection, than they are when in the midst of the heat and turmoil of business, and likely to be disturbed half a dozen times in the course of a five minutes' conversation. But although our income had at the end of our first financial year actually increased, I was careful not to increase our expenditure as regards the housekeeping in any one particular. For I had learnt, as you will do, if you follow out the hints I have herein given, that with care and determination (those great factors towards all success) to succeed, it is comparatively easy, not only to live, but to live well—a very different matter—and to keep up appearances upon £300 a a year!

APPENDIX

A LIST of the cheap and good shopping neighbourhoods in the west and south-west districts:—

For Kensington Proper.—The High Street, Notting Hill Gate and King Street, Hammersmith.

South Kensington.—That part of Fulham Road which lies between Drayton Gardens and Hollywood Road.

For Chelsea.—The King's Road.

For West Kensington.—King Street, Hammersmith.

For Fulham.—The North End Road.

For Knightsbridge.—Brompton Road.

For Earl's Court.—The Kensington end of the Earl's Court Road.

For Ladbroke Grove and North Kensington.—High Street, Notting Hill Gate for preference.

For Chiswick and Bedford Park.—King Street, Hammersmith.

NOTE.—I am aware that the above list might be very largely—almost indefinitely—extended, but I am adhering to my rule of only writing of that which I know.

INDEX

A

B

C

D

E

F

G

M

H

I

J

L

M

N

O

P

T

V

W

For EU product safety concerns, contact us at Calle de José Abascal, 56–1°, 28003 Madrid, Spain or eugpsr@cambridge.org.

www.ingramcontent.com/pod-product-compliance
Ingram Content Group UK Ltd.
Pitfield, Milton Keynes, MK11 3LW, UK
UKHW012342130625
459647UK00009B/484